ULTIMATE DINOSAUR

**LONDON, NEW YORK,
MELBOURNE, MUNICH, AND DELHI**

For Tall Tree Ltd.
Editors Jon Richards, Camilla Hallinan
Designer Ed Simkins

For DK India
Senior editor Kingshuk Ghoshal
Senior art editor Govind Mittal
Editors Rashmi Rajan, Surbhi N. Kapoor
Art editors Mahipal Singh, Shipra Jain
Picture researcher Sumedha Chopra
Senior DTP designer Jagtar Singh
DTP designers Bimlesh Tiwary, Nand Kishore Acharya
Managing editor Alka Thakur Hazarika
Managing art editor Romi Chakraborty
CTS manager Balwant Singh
Production manager Pankaj Sharma

For DK London
Senior editor Rob Houston
Senior art editor Phillip Letsu
Production editor Adam Stoneham
US editor Margaret Parrish
Production controller Mary Slater
Jacket designers Mark Cavanagh, Ivy Roy
Jacket editor Manisha Majithia
Jacket design development manager Sophia M. Tampakopoulos Turner
Publisher Andrew Macintyre
Associate publishing director Liz Wheeler
Art director Philip Ormerod
Publishing director Jonathan Metcalf

First American edition, 2013
Published in the United States by
DK Publishing, 345 Hudson Street, New York, New York 10014
15 16 17 10 9 8 7 6 5 4
008—184808—April/13

Copyright © 2013 Dorling Kindersley Limited
All rights reserved

A catalog record for this book is available from the Library of Congress.
ISBN: 978-1-4654-0587-6

DK books are available at special discounts when purchased in bulk for sales promotions, premiums, fund-raising, or educational use.
For details, contact: DK Publishing Special Markets, 345 Hudson Street, New York, New York 10014 or SpecialSales@dk.com.

Printed and bound by Leo, China
Discover more at
www.dk.com

ULTIMATE DINOSAUR

Written by:

Douglas Palmer

3

Senses and behavior

4

The end

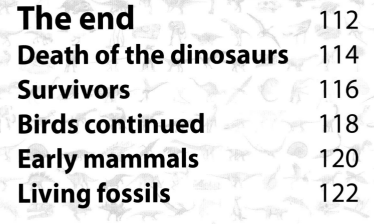

Contents

CLASH OF THE TITANS
Never has nature been so red in tooth and claw as when giant dinosaurs roamed the Mesozoic world. None was more terrifying than tyrannosaurs such as *Tarbosaurus,* the most powerful predator in Cretaceous China.

World of the dinosaurs

WHAT ARE DINOSAURS?

Dinosaurs form a unique group of extinct reptiles that appeared on Earth about 230 million years ago. Their skeletons show certain features, especially the bone structure of the hips, legs, feet, and skulls that made them different from other reptiles. There were two groups of dinosaur, differing in the structure of their hip bones. Today, we know about more than 1,000 different species of dinosaur. We know that the dinosaurs are descended from earlier archosaur reptiles, but their exact origins are still unclear. Although most dinosaurs are extinct, their bird descendants survive.

Pillarlike dinosaur limbs supported their heavy bodies

Crocodile limbs bend to partly support the body

Lizard limbs stick out sideways from the body

▲ STANCE

One of the most distinctive features of the dinosaurs was the structure of the limb bones and the way these were attached to the rest of the skeleton. The limbs of most reptiles stick out sideways from the body. This position would not have supported heavy dinosaur bodies. They could only evolve to such great sizes because their upright limbs were positioned directly under the body. This stance also made dinosaurs quite agile.

▶ DISCOVERY AND NAMING

By 1840, fossils of several large reptiles had been discovered in England, including *Megalosaurus* and *Iguanodon*. English paleontologist Richard Owen named this group of extinct animals "dinosaurs," meaning "terrible lizards," because of their great size. In 1851, Owen built the first life-sized dinosaur models.

Megalosaurus model, London, England

▼ LIZARD-HIPPED DINOSAURS

The pelvis of the lizard-hipped saurischia, which include the plant-eating sauropodomorphs and the meat-eating theropods, had a pubis bone pointing forward.

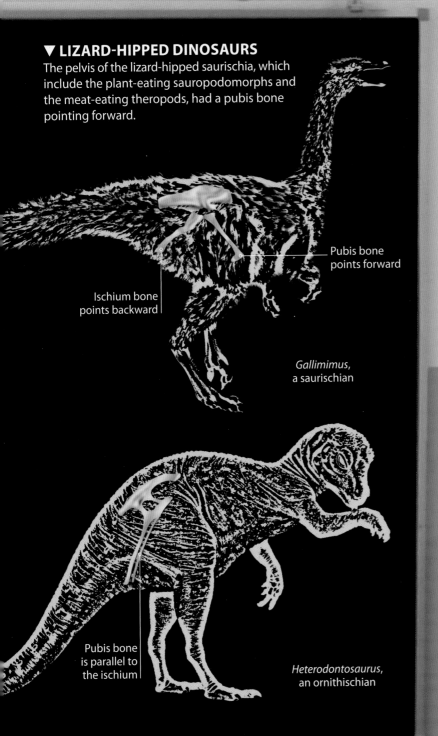

Pubis bone points forward

Ischium bone points backward

Gallimimus, a saurischian

Pubis bone is parallel to the ischium

Heterodontosaurus, an ornithischian

▼ FAMILY TREE

Dinosaurs form a group of archosaur reptiles that splits into the ornithischia and the saurischia. The plant-eating ornithischians include thyreophorans (including stegosaurs and ankylosaurs), ornithopods, and marginocephalians (including ceratopsians and pachycephalosaurs). The saurischians include plant-eating sauropodomorphs (including sauropods and prosauropods), meat-eating theropods, and their descendants—the birds.

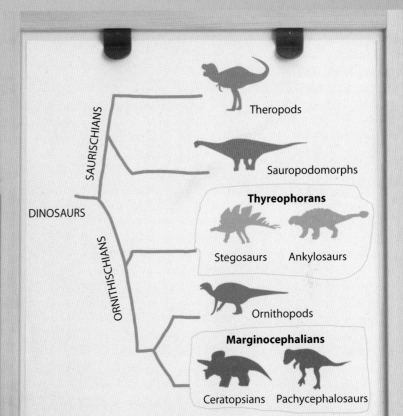

SAURISCHIANS

Theropods

Sauropodomorphs

DINOSAURS

Thyreophorans

Stegosaurs   Ankylosaurs

ORNITHISCHIANS

Ornithopods

Marginocephalians

Ceratopsians   Pachycephalosaurs

▲ BIRD-HIPPED DINOSAURS

In the bird-hipped ornithischia, the pubis bone of the pelvis pointed backward, parallel to the ischium, as in that of a bird. They were all plant-eaters with an extra beaklike bone in front of the lower jaw. This group included the stegosaurs, ankylosaurs, ornithopods, ceratopsians, and pachycephalosaurs.

THE CHANGING WORLD

Ever since Earth's formation 4.6 billion years ago, our planet has experienced constant change. Earth's surface has seen the creation of oceans, continents, and the atmosphere; the rise and fall of volcanoes and mountains; and the transformation of climates. In this changing environment, life on Earth is always changing, too. Over a period of more than 3.5 billion years, billions of life-forms, from microbes to mammoths, have emerged, evolved, and died out. Dinosaurs are one part of that long and ongoing story.

▶ VOLCANIC BOUNDARIES

Volcanoes often mark the boundaries of the rocky plates that make up Earth's outer crust. Heat flowing from within the planet constantly pushes these plates around. Over time, these movements can open and close oceans and push the continents together to build vast mountain chains. Clouds of volcanic ash spreading through the Earth's atmosphere also alter the climate.

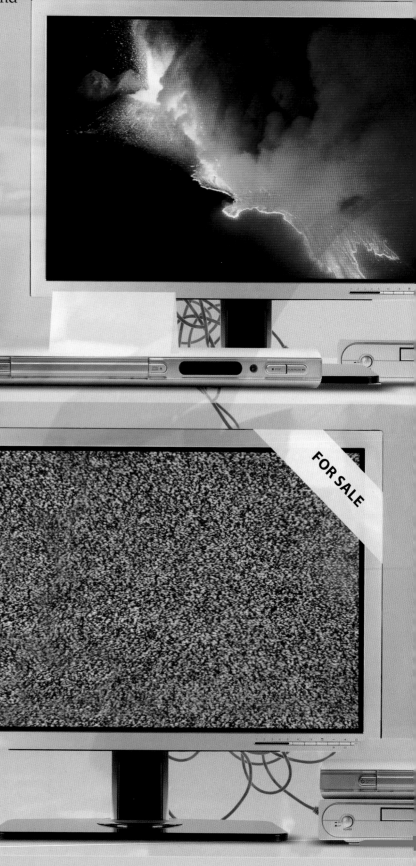

Triassic 252–201 million years ago   Jurassic 201–145 million years ago

Cretaceous 145–66 million years ago   Present day

▲ BREAKING UP

Scientists divide Earth's history into periods. The time of the dinosaurs is called the Mesozoic Era and is split into three periods. In the Triassic Period, the landmasses on the Earth's crust, which had formed a single supercontinent called Pangaea, began to pull apart. Animals were cut off and evolved distinct new species. By the Jurassic Period, there were two continents with warm climates and vast, shallow seas flooding some of the land. In the Cretaceous Period, the continents continued to break apart, some shifting toward the poles and others toward the equator. Today's seven continents are still moving.

FOR SALE

◀ ICE AGES

The evolution of life on Earth has been disrupted by several ice ages. Each lasted for millions of years as temperatures plunged and ice sheets spread over the land. These glacial phases alternate with warm phases, when melting ice sheets and glaciers lead to rising sea levels, and rapid climate change alters habitats and the life they support.

SOLD

▶ MASS EXTINCTION

Over the last 600 million years, the history of life has been dramatically altered by several mass extinctions in which huge numbers of species died out. Rapid climate change was the likely cause of most of these events, but the mass extinction at the end of the Cretaceous Period was triggered by the impact of an asteroid from space crashing into Earth.

▲ FIRST VERTEBRATES

The first vertebrates (animals with backbones) appeared about 530 mya in the Cambrian Period. One of the earliest vertebrates was the fishlike *Haikouichthys* from China. Just 1 in (2.5 cm) long, it had eyes and could swim, but lacked jaws and teeth. It sucked up microscopic food using its simple mouth.

ORDOVICIAN
485–443 mya

SILURIAN
443–419 mya

TREE-SIZED PLANTS ▶

Plants made the move onto land in the Ordovician Period. Early plants were low-growing mosslike organisms. Plants grew larger and more upright in the Silurian Period. By the Late Devonian Period, tree-sized plants, such as *Archaeopteris*, had evolved, but plants at this time were still confined to low-lying, wet environments.

DEVONIAN
419–359 mya

CAMBRIAN
541–485 mya

◀ ANIMALS ON LAND

The first four-limbed animals, or tetrapods, emerged in the Late Devonian Period and were water-dwellers. By the Carboniferous Period, tetrapods had made the move to land. Early land-dwelling tetrapods included *Westlothiana*, a small insect-eating, lizardlike, primitive reptile.

▼ EARLY LIFE

In Precambrian times, life was mostly single-celled, microscopic, and completely confined to the oceans. A long, slow phase of evolution eventually saw the appearance of many-celled organisms, such as this 1.2-billion-year-old red alga *Bangiomorpha*. From these, even more complex organisms emerged over time.

PRECAMBRIAN
4.6 bya–541 mya
(million years ago)

TIMELINE

Dinosaurs dominated our planet for about 160 million years–far longer than humans have been around. Yet this is just a fraction of time in the long story of life on Earth. Life has existed for at least 3.5 billion years, but for the first 3 billion it was microscopic and confined to the oceans. Organisms grew larger and more complex in the Cambrian Period. Primitive plants first moved onto land in the Ordovician Period. They were followed in the Devonian Period by the first land-dwelling vertebrates, paving the way for the rise of the dinosaurs in the Triassic Period.

START

**4.6 billion years ago
(bya)**

AGE OF TETRAPODS ▶

When land-dwelling vertebrates began to lay waterproof eggs, they no longer had to return to water to breed. In the Permian Period, several groups of land-dwelling tetrapods evolved and died out. These included synapsids, such as this sail-backed *Dimetrodon*, which grew to more than 13 ft (4 m) tall.

▼ RISE OF HUMANS

Humans and chimps are primates and share a mammal ancestor that lived about 6 mya in Africa. Just 3¼ ft (1 m) tall, the plant-eating *Sahelanthropus* from the southern Sahara dates from that time and may be an ancestor of modern humans.

QUATERNARY
2.6 mya–present

Skull fossil of *Sahelanthropus*

PERMIAN
299–252 mya

TRIASSIC
252–201 mya

NEOGENE
23–2.6 mya

CARBONIFEROUS
359–299 mya

PALEOGENE
66–23 mya

DAWN OF THE DINOSAURS ▶

The Permian Period ended with a mass extinction, when many species died out at the same time. Life slowly recovered in the Triassic Period with the further evolution of many kinds of tetrapod. New groups of marine reptiles emerged, as well as land-dwelling archosaur reptiles. From the archosaurs came the first crocodile-like animals, the first pterosaurs, and the first dinosaurs, such as *Eoraptor*.

FIRST FLOWERING PLANTS ▶

The Early Cretaceous Period saw the evolution of the first flowering plants. They were small and grew in wet environments. By the end of this period, however, flowering plants had colonized a range of habitats. They included large shrub- and tree-sized plants, such as magnolias, which were pollinated by flying insects.

JURASSIC
201–145 mya

◀ RAPID EVOLUTION

Many groups of dinosaur of all sizes evolved in the Jurassic Period, including small, feathered theropods that were the ancestors of the first birds. While dinosaurs and other reptiles dominated life on land and in the oceans, small mammals, such as *Sinoconodon*, were also emerging.

CRETACEOUS
145–66 mya

LIFE BEFORE THE DINOSAURS

Evolution is a slow process. After about 3 billion years of Precambrian evolution in the sea, life eventually emerged on land in the Ordovician Period, about 450 million years ago. But it took another 100 million years before the first backboned animals emerged from the waters in the Late Devonian Period. Another 120 million years after that, the first dinosaurs appeared in the Late Triassic Period, which was 230 million years ago.

Flat, streamlined skull typical of a fast-swimming predator

Eight webbed fingers on each paddlelike forelimb, used more for swimming than walking

Acanthostega was 3¼ ft (1 m) long

Long, finned tail rippled from side to side to propel *Acanthostega*

Long jaws lined with two rows of sharp teeth

Eyes placed high on skull gave this aquatic predator an upward and sideways view

▲ EARLY AMPHIBIAN

Fishlike vertebrates (backboned animals) arose in Cambrian seas about 530 mya. Some developed limbs with fingers and toes in the Late Devonian Period and became the first tetrapods—animals with four feet. Even then, tetrapods such as *Acanthostega* were still water-dwelling but had lungs that they used for breathing air. Only later did their legs become suited to walking on land.

◄ FIRST REPTILE

The 8-in- (20-cm-) long, lizardlike *Hylonomus* is the first known true reptile. Fossil remains from Late Carboniferous Canada, 312 mya, were found trapped inside hollow tree stumps. Evidently, it was land-dwelling and, unlike the amphibians, probably laid its eggs on land instead of in the water. Its jaws were packed with small, sharp teeth and it most likely fed on insects and other small arthropods.

Lizardlike limb stuck out sideways from the body

◄ BACK TO THE WATER

In Late Carboniferous Kansas, just over 300 mya, *Spinoaequalis* was one of the first reptiles to return to living in water—where its tetrapod ancestors had lived. It was 10 in (25 cm) long, with long-toed, sprawling legs, and a deep, flat tail that was a powerful tool for swimming. Fossilized along with some marine fish, it may have ventured downstream into the sea. However, it still had to return to land to lay its eggs.

Long, lizardlike legs and toes

▼ OPHIACODON

Growing to 10 ft (3 m) long, *Ophiacodon* was one of the largest Late Carboniferous tetrapods, weighing up to 110 lb (50 kg). Its sprawling legs were powerfully built, so it could make rapid lunges to catch fish. Its skull structure shows that *Ophiacodon* was a synapsid—a member of a group of tetrapods from which the mammals would evolve in the Triassic Period, 100 million years later.

With its sprawling gait, *Ophiacodon* resembled a crocodile

Long, crocodile-like jaws lined with 166 sharp teeth

▼ EFFIGIA

Living on dry land alongside early dinosaurs in Late Triassic US (210 mya), *Effigia* was up to 10 ft (3 m) long, sleek, bipedal (moving on its two hind legs), and fast. It looked very like theropod dinosaurs such as *Coelophysis* (see pages 16–17), but it was, in fact, a member of the large group of older reptiles that gave rise to dinosaurs, crocodiles, turtles, and pterosaurs.

Like the theropods, *Effigia* held up its long tail for balance on the move

TRIASSIC WORLD

In the Triassic Period, 252–201 million years ago, plant and animal life began to recover from the catastrophic mass extinction at the end of the Permian Period. Across the Pangaea supercontinent, which was hot and largely barren, the rise of the archosaurs ("ruling reptiles") included the first dinosaurs appearing on the land and pterosaurs in the skies. Crocodiles emerged, and turtles and ichthyosaurs cruised the oceans. Alongside these reptiles, the very first mammals also evolved.

❶ VEGETATION
Many groups of plant were wiped out in the end-Permian extinction, but there were survivors, including club mosses, such as these *Pleuromeia*. Among the newly evolving vegetation were new kinds of fern and seedplant, including

❷ MIXOSAURUS
The Early Triassic *Mixosaurus* was one of the earliest and most primitive of the ichthyosaurs, a new group of ocean-going reptiles. With a streamlined, dolphinlike body, it was fully adapted to life as a fast-swimming predator.

❸ ENCRINUS
This Triassic sea lily was actually an animal and the last surviving member of a large group of crinoid—most died out in the end-Permian extinction. It lived attached to the seafloor and filtered food particles from the

❹ COELOPHYSIS

Coelophysis was a 10-ft-(3-m-) long, birdlike predator that ran on its long hind legs. It was one of the earliest of the theropod dinosaurs and evolved in the Late Triassic Period from earlier archosaur reptiles, which at first

❺ EUDIMORPHODON

The Late Triassic *Eudimorphodon* is one of the most primitive and oldest known of the pterosaurs, a group of flying reptiles that evolved from earlier archosaurs and dominated the skies of the Mesozoic Era.

❻ POSTOSUCHUS

Growing to more than 13 ft (4 m) long, *Postosuchus* was a medium-sized predator with a massive head and jaws. Although it resembled large theropod dinosaurs, it belonged to a group of Late Triassic archosaurs from which evolved the

JURASSIC WORLD

Two hundred million years ago, the beginning of the Jurassic Period saw the Pangaea supercontinent split into two new continents. Oceans spread, deserts shrank, but global temperatures remained high. Increasingly diverse environments on land and in the sea gave rise to new kinds of plant and animal life. With reptiles dominating the land, seas, and skies, the dinosaurs included the largest land animals ever to have lived—the plant-eating sauropods.

❶ CRYOLOPHOSAURUS

At 20 ft (6 m) long, *Cryolophosaurus* was the largest of the Early Jurassic theropod predators. This dinosaur lived in Antarctica, which was ice-free and forested at the time but still had long, dark winter nights.

❷ SINOCONODON

Bridging the Late Triassic and Early Jurassic periods, *Sinoconodon* was one of the earliest known mammals. This furry, nocturnal predator was 12 in (30 cm) long and had a slim snout but a powerful bite.

❸ BRACHIOSAURUS

By the end of the Jurassic Period, giant plant-eating sauropods were widespread across North America, Europe, and Africa. The Late Jurassic *Brachiosaurus* was 85 ft (26 m) long.

❺ PTERODACTYLUS

The pterosaurs peaked in the Jurassic Period, increasing in number and diversity. *Pterodactylus* had a wingspan of 3¼ ft (1 m). The supremacy of pterosaurs, the largest creatures ever to fly, lasted until the rise of the birds.

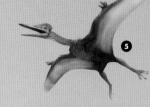

❹ CYLINDROTEUTHIS

Fossils of the squidlike *Cylindroteuthis* are known from around the world, showing how interconnected the oceans were in the Early Jurassic Period.

❻ STEGOSAURUS

Thanks to their bony back plates, stegosaurs—including *Stegosaurus*—are among the best-known groups of plant-eating dinosaur. They were thought to live solely in North America until the recent discovery of a specimen in Portugal.

❼ LIOPLEURODON

This 33-ft- (10-m-) long predator belonged to a group of marine reptile called the pliosaurs. Fossils found in Jurassic rock across Europe and Russia show that a vast sea stretched across the region.

CRETACEOUS WORLD

In the Cretaceous Period, which began 145 million years ago, the modern world slowly began to emerge as the Atlantic Ocean widened and continents gradually moved toward their present positions. Vast shallow seas full of marine life covered low-lying parts of the continents. Temperatures were cooler than before but warmer than today, and life was abundant even at the poles, which were still ice-free. Dinosaurs and the other dominant reptiles continued to flourish—until the Mesozoic Era was brought to an abrupt end 66 million years ago.

❶ VEGETATION

From the Early Cretaceous Period onward, the already varied plants of the Mesozoic Era were joined by flowering plants and by dense forests filled with new kinds of trees.

❷ IBEROMESORNIS

Although primitive birds first appeared in the Late Jurassic Period, more modern birds with short tails and toothless beaks, such as *Iberomesornis*, did not evolve until the Early Cretaceous Period.

❸ VEGAVIS

Vegavis fossils from Antarctica show that by Late Cretaceous times, the ancestors of present-day ducklike waterfowl had evolved.

❹ SINODELPHYS

Sinodelphys was a mouse-sized mammal from Early Cretaceous China. It belonged to an insect-eating group of primitive marsupials that gave birth to tiny babies, which then continued to develop in their mother's pouch.

❺ ARCHAEANTHUS

Flowering plants appeared in the Early Cretaceous Period and became the most diverse group of plants on land. They produced pollen and fruits. *Archaeanthus* had large, magnolia-like flowers.

❻ MUTTABURRASAURUS

This distinctive-looking ornithopod was an Early Cretaceous plant-eater from Australia. *Muttaburrasaurus* had a large, hollow bulge on its snout, which it may have used to create honking sounds.

❼ CYCADEOIDEA

Found across Jurassic and Cretaceous North America and Europe, these cycadlike plants had stocky, barrel-like trunks, a crown of tough, pinnate (feather-shaped) leaves, and seed-bearing cones.

❽ SCAPHITES

Known from fossils of its coiled shell, the ammonite *Scaphites* inhabited oceans across the Cretaceous world. Like all ammonites alive at the time, it died out in the mass extinction at the end of the Cretaceous Period.

DINOSAUR EVOLUTION

Between the Late Triassic and the end of the Cretaceous Period, the dinosaurs evolved from a group of reptiles known as archosaurs into the dominant life-forms on land. Fossil evidence for more than 1,000 species shows that dinosaurs ranged from turkey-sized insect-eaters to the largest and most-ferocious land animals that have ever lived.

Feathered wings and a large breastbone made this Late Cretaceous seabird a strong flyer

Ichthyornis

This dinosaur lived in Late Cretaceous North America

Saurolophus

Deinosuchus

This Late Cretaceous giant was five times larger than any present-day crocodile

▲ WINNERS AND LOSERS

Today, the group of archosaur reptiles from which the dinosaurs evolved is represented by crocodiles and alligators. These large water-dwelling reptiles survived extinction and are still highly successful predators. The only living descendants of the dinosaurs are the birds—they first appeared in the Jurassic Period and now rule the skies.

▶ ARCHOSAUR LINK

The Early Triassic reptile *Euparkeria* links the early reptiles of the Paleozoic Era to the ruling archosaurs and their dinosaur descendants in the Mesozoic Era. This small predator was just 2 ft (60 cm) long and had both primitive archosaur and more advanced dinosaur-like features, such as long back legs, which allowed it to stand upright at times.

Euparkeria

Euparkeria was one of the earliest bipedal reptiles, capable of moving on two legs

Herrerasaurus

▲ EARLY DINOSAUR

One of the first dinosaurs, *Herrerasaurus* lived about 230 million years ago in Late Triassic Argentina. It was a highly active, theropod-like predator, with large eyes and some long, sharp teeth at the front of its mouth. This 16-ft- (5-m-) long saurischian was small for a dinosaur but larger than most other land predators at the time.

Long-legged, long-footed *Herrerasaurus* was bipedal and fast

Long, flexible neck

Plateosaurus could rear up on its hind legs to reach leaves

Plateosaurus skeleton

▲ EARLY PLANT-EATER

Plateosaurus was one of the earliest and most primitive of the long-necked, quadrupedal (four-legged), and sauropod-like plant-eating dinosaurs. Like most of the early dinosaurs, it was relatively small—26 ft (8 m) long at most. It lived in western Europe 220–210 million years ago.

EARLY ORNITHISCHIAN ▶

Heterodontosaurus was an early ornithischian dinosaur and lived in South Africa 200–190 million years ago during the Early Jurassic Period. Only 3¼ ft (1 m) long, this plant-eater was another small dinosaur. This supports the theory, known as Cope's Rule, that new kinds of animal tend to be small compared with the species that evolve from them. Later dinosaurs included some real giants.

Heterodontosaurus

EORAPTOR

The fast-running *Eoraptor* first appeared in the Late Triassic Period. This small theropod was a predator, 3¼ ft (1 m) long, but it probably spent as much time avoiding larger archosaur predators as it did hunting for its own food. *Eoraptor* lived in the densely wooded river valleys of Argentina, where the weather changed greatly with the seasons.

▼ MIXED DIET

Eoraptor's name means "dawn thief," but this little dinosaur was not just a predator. Although most of its teeth were typical of a meat-eater, some of the teeth in its lower jaw were typical of a plant-eater. This means that it was probably an omnivore that ate both small animals and plants.

Long, serrated teeth used for slicing through meat

▶ HANDS

Eoraptor's muscular arms were half as long as its legs. It had long hands with five fingers. The three largest fingers had claws, useful for grabbing prey.

▶ FEET

Eoraptor ran on its two long hind legs, each of which ended in five-clawed toes. The three middle toes were much larger and stronger than the other two.

▲ EOCURSOR

Another early dinosaur sharing the Late Triassic world with *Eoraptor* was *Eocursor* ("dawn runner"). Although this speedy dinosaur was similar to *Eoraptor* in size and shape, it was one of the earliest ornithischians, and it had the leaf-shaped teeth of a plant-eater. But it also had large, clawed hands, so it may have caught the occasional small animal, too.

▲ EORAPTOR SKULL

Behind the long, teeth-lined jaws, the lightly built skull of *Eoraptor* has large eye sockets set on either side of its snout. Big, sideways-facing eyes gave *Eoraptor* a good all-around view—handy for spotting predators as well as prey.

TYPES OF DINOSAUR

As dinosaurs evolved, they split into two main groups, the ornithischians and saurischians, with different hip structures. From these developed many other groups, which ranged from some of the largest animals ever to have lived on land to tiny, birdlike feathered animals and, finally, the birds themselves. This diversity allowed the dinosaurs to dominate the world's landscapes, but—apart from the birds—they were all wiped out in the mass extinction at the end of the Cretaceous Period.

❷ EUOPLOCEPHALUS
Ankylosaurs, such as the Late Cretaceous *Euoplocephalus*, were armored plant-eating ornithischians. *Euoplocephalus* grew to 20 ft (6 m) long and was built like a spiked tank.

❸ VULCANODON
The Early Jurassic *Vulcanodon* was a member of a group of plant-eating saurischians called the sauropods. It had a long neck and tail, a bulky body, and four stout legs; but while most sauropods were giants, *Vulcanodon* was only 23 ft (7 m) long.

❶ STEGOSAURUS
The plant-eating stegosaurs were ornithischians. They featured two rows of large bony plates along their backs and pairs of long spines on their tails. The Late Jurassic *Stegosaurus* was the largest, measuring 30 ft (9 m).

26

❹ STYRACOSAURUS

The Late Cretaceous ceratopsians were plant-eating ornithischians with huge neck frills. The frill of *Styracosaurus* had an impressive array of spikes, each 2 ft (60 cm) long.

❺ CARCHARODONTOSAURUS

Measuring 39 ft (12 m) in length, *Carcharodontosaurus* was one of the largest predators on land. This saurischian dinosaur belonged to a group of theropods that were distantly related to the tyrannosaurs.

❻ DRYOSAURUS

The ornithopods, such as *Dryosaurus* from the Jurassic, evolved from small, two-legged ornithischians to become one of the most successful and widespread groups of plant-eating dinosaurs.

❼ VELOCIRAPTOR

The theropods were mostly meat-eating saurischians. The Late Cretaceous *Velociraptor* belonged to a group of small, two-legged and feathered theropods called dromaeosaurs. It was an agile predator.

❽ PLATEOSAURUS

Among the earliest groups of saurischians to evolve in the Late Triassic Period were large and long-necked plant-eaters called prosauropods. *Plateosaurus* was 26 ft (8 m) long.

❾ MICRORAPTOR

Some feathered dromaeosaurs, such as the tiny Early Cretaceous *Microraptor*, had long feathers on their arms and legs. They may have been capable of gliding, but they could not flap their wings and fly.

❿ CONFUCIUSORNIS

Early Cretaceous *Confuciusornis* was a pigeon-sized early bird that evolved from the dromaeosaurs. It had a toothless beak and a short tail with two long feathers.

27

OTHER PREHISTORIC REPTILES

Many kinds of reptile have evolved and died out in the last 300 million years. In the Permian Period, 299–252 million years ago, reptiles ruled the land. While the first dinosaurs began to appear in the Late Triassic Period, around 230 million years ago, the skies were dominated by the pterosaurs and the oceans were home to marine reptiles such as turtles, nothosaurs, and crocodile-like predators. Only some of these groups survived the mass extinction at the end of the Cretaceous Period, 66 million years ago, but reptiles today include more than 5,600 species of lizard, 3,400 species of snake, 300 species of turtle and tortoise, and 23 species of crocodile and alligator.

❶ PTEROSAURS

The pterosaurs (meaning "winged reptiles") were the first flying vertebrates, and the largest. They dominated Mesozoic skies but died out in the end-Cretaceous extinction. Early Jurassic *Dimorphodon* had a wingspan of 4¾ ft (1.45 m) and snapped up fish and small reptiles.

❷ SYNAPSIDS

Synapsids were the largest group of land-dwelling vertebrate in the Permian Period. They included *Eothyris*, which lived 290–280 mya. This mysterious animal is known only from a single skull. It was a lizardlike carnivore about 12 in (30 cm) long.

❸ CROCODYLOMORPHS

Crocodiles and alligators, such as the enormous Late Cretaceous *Deinosuchus*, belonged to a large group of archosaur reptile known as the crocodylomorphs (meaning "crocodile-shaped"), which survived the end-Cretaceous extinction.

❹ TURTLES

Turtles, tortoises, and terrapins are known as the Testudines because of their shells—*testudo* is Latin for "shell." There were many more species on land and in the water in the past than there are today. Late Cretaceous *Protostega* was 10 ft (3 m) long.

❺ NOTHOSAURS

Thrashing their long tails from side to side, these fish-hunting reptiles prowled through shallow coastal seas in the Triassic Period. One of the largest, *Nothosaurus*, grew to 13 ft (4 m) long and came ashore to rest and breed.

29

MOSASAURUS

In the Late Cretaceous Period, mosasaurs formed one of several groups of large, marine (sea-dwelling) reptiles that dominated the oceans. These were not dinosaurs, but evolved from small land-dwelling lizards that took to the water in search of food. Like the ichthyosaurs and plesiosaurs, the mosasaurs became so well adapted to marine life that they did not return to land to breed, as turtles do. Along with most other marine reptiles, they were wiped out by the mass extinction at the end of the Cretaceous Period, which, among marine reptiles, only the turtles and crocodilians survived.

▼ MEET MOSASAURUS

A terrifying 50 ft (15 m) long, *Mosasaurus* was one of the largest of the mosasaurs and one of the most ferocious predators ever to have lived and hunted in the Earth's oceans. It probably hunted in well lit waters close to the surface. Though adapted to life in the prehistoric seas, with flippers and a long, streamlined body, these carnivores still came to the surface to breathe air.

▶ TEETH

Mosasaurs had different types of teeth, depending on what they ate. Most mosasaurs, such as *Mosasaurus*, were active meat-eating predators with very strong, sharp, conical teeth, like those of a crocodile. Other mosasaurs had shorter, blunter teeth and specialized in crushing shelled mollusks.

Sharp, conical teeth

◀ OPEN WIDE

The skull of a mosasaur called *Plioplatecarpus* had a hingelike structure that opened extra wide. This allowed it to swallow large prey whole, as snakes do. Mosasaurs probably hunted by ambushing their prey, using slow, stealthy movements to approach and then a sudden, swift lunge to grab the unsuspecting victim. Some mosasaur jaw bones show tooth marks and healed fractures, which suggests these animals also fought one another—probably males fighting over females.

▲ TAIL AS PROPELLER

Mosasaurus had a very long tail. It normally swam by slowly rippling its body from side to side, as snakes do, and steering with its two pairs of large, paddlelike limbs. It could also, however, accelerate forward in a brief burst of speed by rapidly thrashing its strong, flattened tail from side to side.

Legs evolved into paddles

▼ GIGANTIC JAW

Mosasaurus was discovered in the 18th century, when miners digging near the town of Maastricht in the Netherlands discovered a spectacular jawbone 3¼ ft (1 m) long. The new creature was named the "Great Beast" of Maastricht. Scientists at the time thought the jaws might have belonged to a crocodile or whale, but mosasaurs are now thought to be related to lizards.

▼ AN UNUSUAL SNOUT

Tylosaurus was another giant mosasaur, up to 36 ft (11 m) long. It had a distinct hard, bony tip to its snout, which may have been used as a ram to stun prey. Some specimens have been found with damaged snouts—perhaps the result of ramming larger prey or fighting with male rivals.

HOW FOSSILS ARE MADE

Dinosaurs disappeared 66 million years ago, long before the first humans appeared. Nearly everything we know about dinosaurs we learn from fossils. Fossils are the remains or traces of plants and animals that have been buried and preseved in rock and then rediscovered and dug up. Only a tiny percentage of past life has been fossilized, because fossil formation—and discovery—requires very particular conditions. And even if plants or animals are preserved as fossils, they are dramatically altered in the process.

Eyes, skin, and other soft tissue usually get eaten or rot and decay

▲ FROM FISH TO FOSSIL
This reconstructed bony fish shows how the process of fossilization almost always involves the loss of some of the animal, as its soft parts decay and the body begins to fall apart. Some pieces may be torn off by scavengers or damaged by ocean currents and waves before the remains can sink to the seabed and get buried by silt. Even if the remains do get buried, the soft parts continue to decay.

Tough bony scales on the body and fins may get preserved

▲ DEATH
When an animal dies, scavengers soon find and feed on the body. It only stands a chance of being well preserved as a fossil if there are no scavengers in the area.

▲ BURIAL
Ideally, the entire body is quickly buried under a layer of sediment, such as mud or silt, before any damage or decay has taken place.

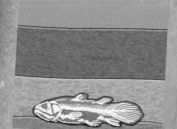

▲ MINERALIZATION
Soft parts decay, leaving only the skeleton. The bones are mineralized by chemicals seeping in from the water and sediment.

Bony skeleton is the
most likely to last
and be fossilized

▲ **PETRIFICATION**
As new layers of sediment
settle on top, mineralization
hardens the skeleton and its
layer of sediment. They are
petrified—turned into rock.

▲ **COMPRESSION**
The weight and pressure
of the new layers of sediment
squash the skeleton flat as
they turn into strata (layers)
of hard rock.

FOSSIL TYPES

Deep under the ground, inside the Earth's crust, enormous weight, pressure, and heat all combine to change sediment into rock. Any plant and animal remains buried in the sediment also become petrified—literally "rocklike"—as fossils. Their burial and fossilization can happen in different ways, and form different kinds of fossil. These fossils continue to shift and change when crustal rock heaves and cracks.

Eye socket still visible in this ichthyosaur's flattened skull

▲ BODY FOSSILS

Fossilized bones and other fragments of long-extinct animals offer exciting clues to the past. Whole skeletons are rare, but vivid. As sediment buried this ichthyosaur's remains, the pressure and weight of the sediment flattened its skeleton. Even so, its bones are still articulated (joined together) and show a powerful swimmer.

▼ TRACKS AND TRACES

Instead of body parts, trace fossils preserve clues left by the body, such as bite marks on bones, footprints, droppings, and nests. These can all reveal the behavior of animals long ago. This trackway of three-toed, birdlike footprints was made by a large theropod dinosaur striding across soft ground.

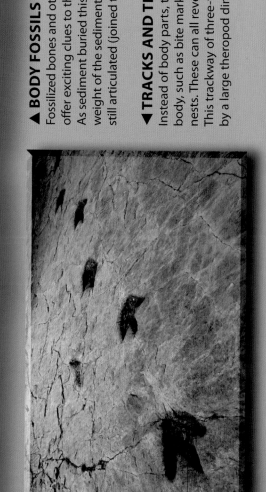

Fossilized footprints of a large theropod dinosaur found in Spain

Flattened and distorted fossils of the "tuning fork" graptolite called *Didymograptus*

Nymphon gracile, a type of living sea spider, closely resembles its ancient relative

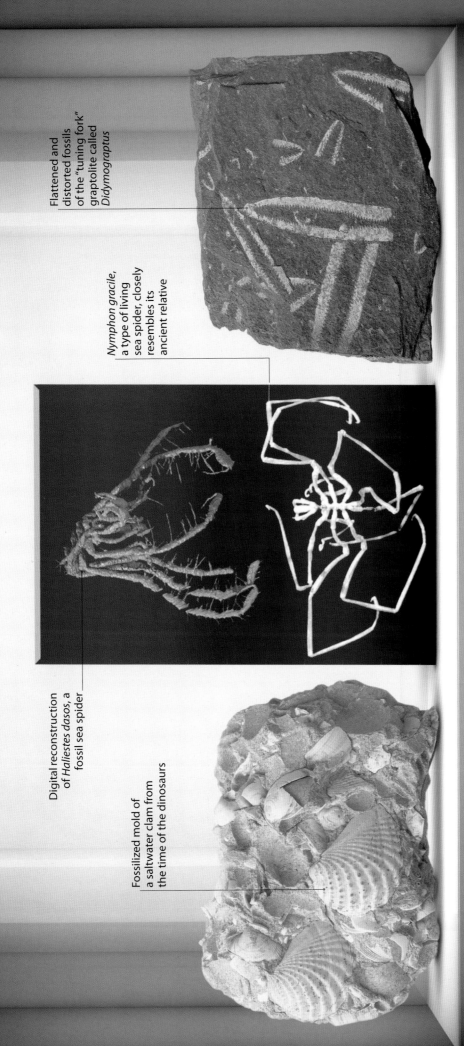

Digital reconstruction of *Haliestes dasos*, a fossil sea spider

Fossilized mold of a saltwater clam from the time of the dinosaurs

▲ MOLDS AND CASTS

During fossilization, even hard parts such as bones and shells can be dissolved by acids in the surrounding sediment. However, if the sediment is very fine-grained, it forms a mold in the exact shape of the fossil's remains before they disappear—as in these sandstone molds of shells. Later on, minerals may refill the hollow left by the remains and form a cast that is an exact replica of the original.

▲ VIRTUAL FOSSILS

Computer technology allows scientists to re-create fossils on screen, using digital images. This image shows a sea spider that lived more than 400 million years ago and was preserved as a hollow mold in sedimentary rock. The mold was scanned to create lots of thin virtual slices through the fossil, which were then digitally combined in 3-D on screen.

▲ DISTORTED FOSSILS

The burial of plant and animal remains not only flattens them, but may also distort them in other ways. This is due to pressure within the Earth's crust, where layers of rock shift, bend, and break during mountain building. Here, fossils of a single species of plankton, more than 400 million years old, have been flattened and squeezed into slightly different shapes.

▼ HEAD-TO-TAIL EVIDENCE

Some animals with armored shells that protect the body, such as this extinct trilobite, have to shed their armor plating again and again in order to grow. Although the process increases the remains available for fossilization, shedding the armor also breaks it up, which is why entire trilobite fossils are relatively rare.

Trilobite shell fossilized in one piece, from head to tail

FOSSIL CLUES

Formed in many different ways, fossils are remarkable survivors that offer valuable clues to life in the past. After lying buried for millions of years, some are dug up but most are exposed when layers of rock are eroded away by weather and glaciers. Then a single tooth may be enough to identify the fossil remains of a long-extinct species, or a single feather may change ideas about how it looked and moved.

Entire articulated (joined) skeleton of *Homeosaurus*, a small Jurassic reptile

Fossil shark's tooth with serrated cutting edge

▲ MADE WITH MINERALS

Hard body parts such as bones, teeth, and shells might seem tough, but they contain chemicals that can decay after death. However, the fossilization process can introduce different minerals into these remains, making them harder and heavier. Mineralized fossils are the most common.

▶ CARBON FEATHERS

Made of a carbon-rich protein called keratin, feathers are some of the toughest animal tissues, so they decay more slowly than flesh or muscle. During fossilization, the keratin is broken down into a charcoallike carbon residue that lasts over time. The discovery of dinosaur fossils with the carbonized remains of feathers has revolutionized our understanding of the evolution of feathers, flight, and the link between dinosaurs and birds.

Long, flight feathers still visible in fossilized *Microraptor*, a dinosaur from Early Cretaceous China

ONITE
:boceras nathorsti
ssic, Kimme

SOFT TISSUES
Hedgehoglike mammal with some of its skin and fur preserved

▲ PLANT TISSUES
Plant tissues vary in strength from tough wood, which can last many years, to flower petals, which may last only a few weeks. As a result, fossilized flowers, such as this 34-million-year-old *Florissantia* from the US, are extremely rare.

Petal-like sepals

▲ SOFT TISSUES
In certain, extremely rare conditions, carbon traces of soft tissues, such as hair and skin, may be preserved, or replaced by other minerals. Dating back 47 million years, oil shales at Messel in Germany provide exceptional preservation of many plants and animals. Some have been found with fossilized hair and even stomach contents.

Preserved tree growth rings

FROM WOOD TO SILICA▶
Wood is made of tough cellulose, but it decays over time. During fossilization, minerals called silicas can seep into the wood and gradually replace the cellulose. As the silica hardens, it preserves the details of the wood's cellular structure. This form of mineralization allows experts to identify the original plant.

▲ INSECTS
Insects are the most common living organisms, but their fossils are quite rare because only some species have body parts that are tough enough to survive fossilization. Butterfly and moth fossils complete with wings, such as this 30-million-year-old specimen from France, are very rare.

Pyrite internal mold of an ammonite

▲ PYRITE REPLICA
Pyrite, or "fool's gold," is an iron sulfide mineral produced by certain microbes in muds and other sediments. During fossilization, pyrite crystals grow inside shells and bones and create replicas of the structures they replace. This is another form of mineralization.

UNCOVERING FOSSILS

Most of the species of animal and plant that have existed on Earth are now extinct. We know about many of them through the fossilized remains of their bodies. So far, paleontologists have only found a tiny fraction of the fossils that lie buried in rock, so we are learning about new species all the time. Small fossils, such as shells, are sometimes found whole. The fossilized remains of larger organisms usually have to be excavated from the rock. This can be a long and difficult process.

▶ EXCAVATION

Working on a tilted surface, paleontologists at the Dinosaur National Monument in Utah painstakingly uncover scattered dinosaur bones that are embedded in hard, sedimentary rock. The fossils include the remains of several large Jurassic sauropods.

▼ TOOLS

Sedimentary rocks can be as hard as concrete and it may be necessary to use rock saws, hammers, and chisels to excavate the fossils. Great care has to be taken to avoid damage to the bones.

▼ X-RAY

An X-ray image can reveal the details of a fossil that is totally encased in rock, such as this *Confuciusornis*. Paleontologists use the information from the X-ray as a guide so that they can separate the rock in a way that does not damage the fossil.

◄ CT SCAN

X-rays have been used to build a computer image of this *Lambeosaurus* skull. The image allows paleontologists to study the structure of the fossil skull in detail. They can rotate the image and look at cross-sections of the insides of the fossil.

PIECING THINGS TOGETHER

The remains of plants and animals rarely stay intact after they die. The processes of fossilization break up and scatter even the tough hard parts, such as skeletons and shells. Normally, all a paleontologist is left with is a mixed-up collection of fragments or isolated fossils that may be widely scattered throughout a rock. The collector has first to excavate and recover as many pieces as possible and then reassemble the original organism from the pieces. This can be especially difficult with long-extinct organisms whose original body form may not be known.

◀ **THE WHOLE STORY**
Complete fossil remains of vertebrates, such as *Citipati*—a feathered dinosaur from Late Cretaceous Mongolia—are extremely rare. Rarer still are fossils that preserve an animal in a lifelike position, such as guarding its nest and eggs. This exceptional fossil was amazingly well preserved because the animal refused to leave its nest in a sandstorm that rapidly suffocated and buried it.

◀ PLANT REMAINS

Scientists recognize living flowering plants by the shape of their flowers, the number and shape of their petals, and their reproductive organs, which produce seeds. However, flowers are normally very delicate and their fossils, such as those of *Florissantia* 56–23 mya, are especially rare.

Ulodendron
(fossil stem with spiral leaf cushions)

Lepidodendron
(fossil bark)

Stigmaria
(fossil root-like stems)

Lepidostrobophyllum
(fossil cone scale)

Lepidostrobus
(fossil cone)

NAMING FOSSILS ▶

When different parts of an unknown species are found at different sites by different people they may be given different names. It took a while for scientists to realize that these five fossils all belonged to the same type of tree— *Lepidodendron*, from Carboniferous coal swamps 359–299 mya.

Lepidodendron

Thumb spike on nose, like a rhinoceros

◀ EARLY MISTAKES

In the 1800s, some intriguing fossils were first recognized as belonging to a new group of animal called dinosaurs—a name that means "terrible lizards." But the fossils' gigantic size and shape led early paleontologists to believe that dinosaurs were more like elephants and rhinoceroses than reptiles, as in this early reconstruction of an *Iguanodon*.

PTEROSAUR
Scientists have found fossilized bones of creatures such as this flying pterosaur, *Pterodactylus*. Using their knowledge of living animals' bodies, they can work out how the pterosaurs must have looked.

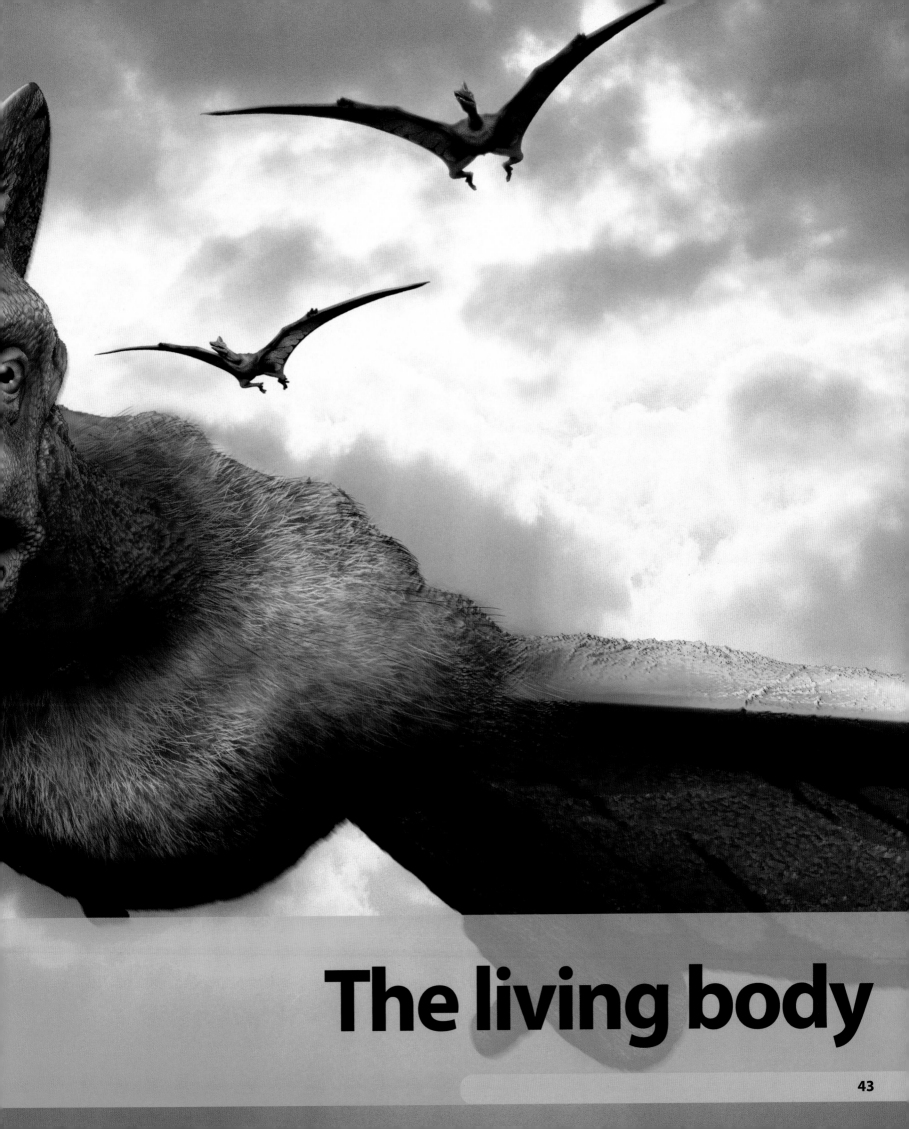

The living body

SKELETONS

Without a supporting skeleton, dinosaurs and other vertebrate animals would be mounds of flesh, unable to move around. Skeletons provide an essential internal framework for holding the body organs together and for anchoring muscles at joints that enable the body to move. Fossil skeletons provide essential clues to how very different dinosaurs looked and moved—some on two hind legs, some on all fours.

▼ HERRERASAURUS

Late Triassic *Herrerasaurus*, one of the earliest dinosaurs, had the skeleton of a typical saurischian, theropod-like predator. Its 17-ft- (5-m-) backbone and small, slender ribs supported a slim body, with a long tail and long, powerful hind legs. A short, powerful neck carried a strong skull and jaws. This was clearly a predator that could outrun and overpower its prey.

Saurischian hip bones

Skull lightened by large holes

Short arms with long, clawed fingers

▼ TYRANNOSAURUS REX

This famous dinosaur has the typical yet awesome skeleton of a large theropod. Its strong backbone stretched 40 ft (12 m) from head to tail. Some of the vertebrae had holes to lessen their weight. So did the enormous skull, whose jaw structure shows that *T. rex* had a stronger bite than any other animal. The massive body was lifted 13 ft (4 m) high at its hips by heavily muscled long hind legs.

Peculiarly short arms with three sharply clawed fingers

Long powerful hind legs carried one of the largest-ever terrestrial carnivores

▶ DIPLODOCUS

Reaching 85 ft (25 m) in length and supporting a bodyweight of up to 17½ tons (16 metric tons), the skeleton of the sauropod *Diplodocus* was exceptionally strong yet relatively light. The vertebrae of the incredibly long neck and tail had hollows that made them lighter. In between, a deep rib cage protected the plant-eater's huge belly, and the body's bulk was supported on massive hind legs and longer front legs.

15 vertebrae in the neck

Small skull with peglike teeth

▶ STEGOSAURUS

The distinctive array of large bony plates along the backbone makes *Stegosaurus* one of the best-known of the large, heavily built, and armored dinosaurs. From its small head to the tip of its tail armed with two pairs of tall spikes, this plant-eating ornithischian grew to 30 ft (9 m) long. The backbone arched over long, stout hind legs and shorter front legs, and carried a deep rib cage.

Bony plates each up to 24 in (60 cm) tall

Sharp tail spikes helped in defense

Long tail with up to 40 vertebrae

◀ ORNITHOMIMUS

Ostrichlike *Ornithomimus* was another theropod, with the lightly built skeleton of a fast runner. Its backbone linked a long neck, slim body, and stiff muscular tail, all carried on very long hind legs. Even the foot bones were long, lifting the animal onto its toes for running. Feeding on plants, seeds, and small animals, this 10-ft- (3-m-) long omnivore had a small skull with a toothless beak and large eye sockets.

Long, three-toed, birdlike feet

Tall spines on the backbones for muscle attachment

Chevron (V-shaped) bones strengthened the tail's vertebrae

80 vertebrae in the tail

ELASMOSAURUS

The plesiosaurs were gigantic carnivorous marine reptiles. They included long-necked species with small heads, such as *Elasmosaurus*, and the short-necked pliosaurs with huge heads. In both cases, long flipperlike limbs enabled them to power their massive bodies through the water. These aquatic predators dominated Jurassic and Cretaceous oceans before dying out in the end-Cretaceous extinction.

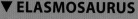

▼ ELASMOSAURUS
Growing to 45 ft (14 m) long, the Late Cretaceous plesiosaur *Elasmosaurus* used its long neck and sharp teeth to grab prey swimming past or dwelling on the seabed. It spent all its life at sea and gave birth to live young under water, but it had to come to the surface to breathe.

▼ SKELETON OF A PLESIOSAUR
Like all long-necked plesiosaurs, *Elasmosaurus* had the skeleton of a fully adapted marine predator, with a wide but streamlined body. Two pairs of paddle-shaped limbs were connected to massive, platelike shoulder and hip bones. The huge muscles that powered the flippers were anchored to these bones.

Neck had more vertebrae than any other animal ever

▼ INSIDE THE STOMACH
The fossilized stomach contents of one short-necked plesiosaur preserved indigestible little hooklets from its squid prey. Other long-necked plesiosaur fossils contain the remains of fish and ammonites, as well as gastroliths (stomach stones), picked from the seabed to help break down food in the stomach.

Pebble   Fish vertebra

▲ INCREDIBLE NECK

With 72 bones in its neck, making up half its body length, *Elasmosaurus* was the marine equivalent of the long-necked sauropods. Swimming slowly over the seabed, it could have reached down to pick prey off the bottom. Some scientists wonder if the neck was also flexible enough to lunge sideways at passing fish.

▲ MIGHTY FLIPPERS

Elasmosaurus had two pairs of enormous, rigid flippers with very long finger bones. The flippers were used to power the huge animal slowly through the water with a combined flapping and rotating motion, as if it were flying.

Fossilized stomach contents of a plesiosaur

▶ BIG BODY, SMALL SKULL

Like sauropod skulls, *Elasmosaurus*'s skull was small in comparison with the rest of its body. The upper part of the skull was fairly flat, and the powerful jaws were lined with long, sharp, outward-pointing teeth. These intermeshed to grip slippery fish, which were then swallowed whole.

Water flowed in through the mouth and out through the nostrils

▶ FEATHERS

Recent finds in China for the Early Cretaceous, pigeon-sized bird called *Confuciusornis* have included carbon traces of soft tissues, such as the different kinds of feathers on the wings and tail. These also preserve some pigment cells that give plumage its color. In 2010, scientific analysis of these microscopic cells revealed that *Confuciusornis* was black, gray, and reddish-brown.

Long pair of tail feathers

SOFT TISSUE

Fossilized soft tissues such as skin and feathers are rare, but they can transform the way we imagine how long-extinct animals might have looked. An exciting series of dinosaur fossils from China, for example, revealed feathery coatings for the first time. These prove the evolutionary link between dinosaurs and birds and show that feathers evolved before flight and were used first for body insulation, display, and camouflage. Other fossils preserve not just skin, but color patterns, too.

Bristles up to 6 in (16 cm) long

▶ SCALY SKIN

Among the many fossil skeletons of *Edmontosaurus* found in North America, some preserve traces of soft tissues, especially its scaly skin. After death, most of the body organs rotted away but some of the skin dried out and fine sand or mud burying the animal molded the pattern of its scales. These skin imprints show small, pointed scales with larger, flatter scales overlapping them.

▶ BRISTLES

This well-preserved specimen of *Psittacosaurus* includes almost the entire skeleton, some patches of scaly skin, and some astonishing bristlelike hollow filaments growing from the tail. Numerous other fossil finds make *Psittacosaurus* one of the best known of the Early Cretaceous ceratopsian dinosaurs, but this one was a complete surprise—no other specimen shows these hollow filaments, and no one is certain what they were used for.

◀ SMOOTH SKIN

Skin traces around fossilized skeletons of the Jurassic ichthyosaur *Stenopterygius* fill in the outline of these marine reptiles, showing a streamlined, dolphin-shaped body with a tall dorsal fin on its back and a deep, crescent-shaped tail fin. The skin traces were actually film produced by a bacterial film that grew over the skin after the animal died and was then preserved as a carbon trace (see pages 36–37).

Preserved upper tail lobe

One of a pair of large front flippers

Toothless beak
like a kingfisher

Preserved skin on body

Broad, ducklike bill
typical of a hadrosaur

This centipede became
trapped in resin about
23 million years ago

▼ **UNDER THE MICROSCOPE**
Amber is fossilized tree resin, which is extremely good at preserving
insects and other small animals. This fossil centipede, accompanied
by several flies, comes from South America and dates back to
the Miocene Epoch, long after the dinosaurs became extinct.
Attracted by the resin's smell as it oozed from the bark,
these little creatures were trapped in the sticky liquid and
preserved as the resin hardened. Amber preserves even the
tiniest and most delicate tissues, such as fly wings,
and minute organisms, such as parasitic microbes.

DINOSAUR GIANTS

Dinosaurs were small at first but over time they grew to gigantic proportions. How large an animal grows depends partly on how its body works. The larger it is, the heavier it gets, and the harder it is for the heart, lungs, and other organs to keep the body running and supply oxygen and nutrients to all its cells. Size may also depend on surroundings, how much food is available, and how many animals are competing for the same type of food. Today's living giants are the whales, whose bodies are supported by ocean water. Fossil records show that some extinct land animals were almost as large. They included the largest of all the dinosaurs found so far.

❶ SPINOSAURUS

This giant, flesh-eating theropod lived in North Africa in the Late Cretaceous Period and had a large fin on its back, supported by bony spines. This unusual feature may have helped control the dinosaur's body temperature. Although its forelimbs were small, its long, crocodile-like jaws were lined with sharp teeth for gripping prey. *Spinosaurus* grew to an estimated length of 50 ft (16 m) and may have weighed 13½ tons (12 metric tons), which makes it the largest known land-dwelling meat-eater.

❷ MONOLOPHOSAURUS

In 1984, the first and only specimen of a giant theropod dinosaur from the Mid-Jurassic Period called *Monolophosaurus* was found in China. About 20 ft (6 m) long, this bipedal meat-eater had a massive skull—one of the largest and oddest of any theropod. It had a large, knobby crest on the top of its head, which was hollow inside and may have been used to produce loud calls.

❸ AMPHICOELIAS

The largest animal ever to walk on Earth might have been the Late Jurassic *Amphicoelias* from North America. But it is only known from a few bones that were found in the 1870s, drawn and described, and then lost! A single upper leg bone is estimated to have been 12 ft (3.7 m) tall. Scaling up from the bones of better known close relatives, *Amphicoelias* is estimated to have been about 160 ft (50 m) long and might have weighed more than 110 tons (100 metric tons), but these measurements are highly speculative.

❹ ARGENTINOSAURUS

Giant plant-eating sauropods are the only land animals that can be compared in size to the whales. *Argentinosaurus*, which lived in the Late Cretaceous Period, is thought to have been 100 ft (30 m) long and weighed up to 77 tons (70 metric tons)—well over 10 times heavier than an elephant. These estimates are based on the incomplete remains found so far. Even with weight-reducing features such as hollow rib bones, it was close to the maximum weight possible for a land animal.

❺ GIANT MAMMALS

The largest mammal ever to live on land was the extinct *Paraceratherium*, which was about 26 ft (8 m) long and weighed about 16½ tons (15 metric tons). The present-day blue whale, *Balaenoptera*, is 100 ft (30 m) long and probably the largest animal of all time. Its heart is the size of a small car.

❻ PRESENT-DAY GIANTS

No living land animals match the dimensions of the dinosaurs. The African elephant, the largest animal on land today, grows up to 13 ft (4 m) tall at the shoulder and weighs up to 6½ tons (6 tons).

Human

51

BAROSAURUS

Towering over almost all other dinosaurs, *Barosaurus* was one of the giant plant-eating sauropods of the Late Jurassic Period and inhabited the thickly vegetated coastal plains of North America. Growing to about 92 ft (28 m) long and weighing up to 20 tons, it had a spectacularly long neck. This helped it reach higher into trees than other sauropods and browse tender new foliage. *Barosaurus* also had a distinctive row of triangular bony plates along its back, from the neck all down the length of its tail; these were possibly used for display or defense.

▼ GIANT SAUROPOD

Barosaurus was heavier than three elephants. Like most sauropods, it needed a massive body to hold its bulky stomach when laden with plant food, which is slow to digest. Because of its enormous weight, the legs were relatively short, although the front legs were longer than the hind ones. It is unlikely that *Barosaurus* could have risen up on its hind legs.

Long tail provided counterbalance to the long neck

Diplodocus skeleton

Short and sturdy hind legs

◄ SUPERSIZED SKELETON

Barosaurus is known from several partial skeletons, which include some limb and back bones but no skulls or foot bones. The back and limb bones are similar to those of the better known *Diplodocus* but differ in enough detail to tell them apart. Three partial skeletons were found at the same site in Utah, which suggests that these animals may have lived in herds.

▼ LONG NECK

Although *Barosaurus* had 16 neck bones and the closely related *Diplodocus* had 15, *Barosaurus*'s neck bones were one-third longer, with some growing up to 3¼ ft (1 m) long. *Barosaurus* could browse treetops 50 ft (15 m) above the ground—the height of a four-story building. Yet this was not the longest sauropod neck—*Mamenchisaurus* may have broken the record with a neck that was 46 ft (14 m) long.

30-ft- (9-m-) long neck allowed *Barosaurus* to reach treetop leaves

▼ MISSING SKULL

Although no fossil remains of a *Barosaurus* skull have been found so far, scientists assume that it would have been like the skull of the similarly sized sauropod *Diplodocus*. If they are right, *Barosaurus* would have had a relatively small but long skull, and jaws with large, peglike teeth at the front of its mouth for stripping leaves from the trees it browsed on.

Long peglike teeth at front for stripping foliage

▲ LONG TAIL

Barosaurus's individual tail bones were shorter than those of *Diplodocus*. Therefore, even though the total number of 80 tail bones was probably the same in both animals, the tail of *Barosaurus* was shorter than that of *Diplodocus*. Nevertheless, the tail was still long enough to crack like a whip and lash out at predators.

Diplodocus skull

TINY DINOSAURS

When we hear the word "dinosaur," we usually think of huge animals that lived long ago. However, this isn't the whole story. The smallest dinosaurs of all are some of the birds that are still alive today. That is because birds evolved from small, theropod dinosaurs in the Late Jurassic Period (see pages 58–59). Even before birds evolved, there were many small dinosaurs no more than 3¼ ft (1 m) long. Scientists have to be careful when they find small fossils because it can be difficulat to tell whether they belonged to a small adult or to the young of a large species.

❶ HUMMINGBIRD

The smallest dinosaurs are the hummingbirds, which are alive today. Most hummingbirds are no more than 5 in (13 cm) long, but some are as small as 2 in (5 cm). Their lightness, size, and wing structure allow them to hover while feeding.

❷ SCUTELLOSAURUS

One of the smallest known dinosaurs, this lightly built ornithischian was about 3¼ ft (1 m) long. It fed on plants and probably walked on its hind legs. Its skin was covered in hundreds of small bony studs.

❸ PSITTACOSAURUS

At some 6½ ft (2 m) long, *Psittacosaurus* was not the smallest dinosaur. But half of its body length was tail, and it was the smallest of the ceratopsians. More than 400 of its fossils have been found.

4 SINOSAUROPTERYX

This tiny dinosaur was just 3¼ ft (1 m) long, about the size of a turkey. Among the theropods, *Sinosauropteryx* had one of the longest tails relative to its body size.

5 LESOTHOSAURUS

This Early Jurassic dinosaur from South Africa was 3¼ ft (1 m) long. *Lesothosaurus* was one of the earliest and most primitive of the plant-eating ornithischians.

6 HETERODONTOSAURUS

This was another small, Early Jurassic ornithischian from South Africa. Just 3¼ ft (1 m) long, *Heterodontosaurus* was primarily a plant-eater, but with long-clawed hands and three different kinds of teeth, it probably ate meat, too.

FEATHERS

Scientists have known about fossil feathers since the 1860s, but for years they thought these finds only came from birds. When the feathered *Archaeopteryx* was first discovered it was classified as a bird even though it had many reptilian features. Since the 1990s, the discovery of many small dinosaurs with featherlike structures shows that feathers first evolved in birdlike theropod dinosaurs, millions of years before they were used by birds for flight.

Long feathered forearms with clawed fingers

▶ MICRORAPTOR

Just 2½ ft (77 cm) long, this tiny Early Cretaceous dromaeosaur had asymmetrical flight feathers, as birds do. Wider on one side, only these asymmetrical feathers create lift for flight. *Microraptor* had them on its legs and long arms and on the end of its long tail. On the ground, however, leg feathers would have made walking and running awkward. But *Microraptor* may have been capable of gliding, swooping from tree to tree to search for food and avoid predators on the ground.

Short arms have large and long clawed fingers, used for grasping prey

Long symmetrical feathers used for display, not for flight

▲ SINOSAUROPTERYX

Discovered in China in 1996, *Sinosauropteryx* caused a sensation. It was the first fossil of a nonflying dinosaur to be found with well preserved traces of feather-related structures. The body was covered with a short, fluffy fuzz, as was the long tail. These simple "proto-feathers" seem very like the down feathers of modern birds and would have provided insulation rather than lift for flight. Just 3¼ ft (1 m) long, *Sinosauropteryx* was almost identical to *Compsognathus*, another small theropod dinosaur. They were both slender, swift-running predators.

▲ CAUDIPTERYX

Another Early Cretaceous theropod called *Caudipteryx* had downy body feathers, while its short arms and long tail carried longer, more evolved, and birdlike plumage. The down probably helped keep *Caudipteryx* warm, but the longer feathers were likely used in display when attracting a mate. Analysis of the skeleton shows that this turkey-sized theropod would not have been able to fly or even glide. Bipedal (moving on two legs), it was built for speed on the ground, chasing insects or fleeing predators.

▶ EVOLUTION OF FEATHERS

The many fossil discoveries from China in the 1990s support the theory that feathers evolved long before flight. Developing from skin scales, the earliest feathers were simple strands like hair. Feathers then became more complex, branching into barbs and developing a central shaft, or rachis. The barbs then subdivided into tiny barbules that meshed together, making feathers stronger and more streamlined. Feathers first provided insulation, camouflage, and display. They then evolved as wing coverings with the asymmetrical feathers necessary for gliding and flapping flight.

Hollow hairlike filament, as found on *Sinosauropteryx*

Multibranched downy tuft of barbs

Feather with a central rachis and barbs

Symmetrical feather with barbs and barbules

Huge curved claws used for gripping and ripping into prey

▲ VELOCIRAPTOR

In 2007, a *Velociraptor* fossil was discovered with small bumps called quill knobs on the arm bones. In living birds, quill knobs carry large feathers, so maybe *Velociraptor* had large feathers on its arms—and on other parts, too. This Late Cretaceous bipedal dromaeosaur was 6½ ft (2 m) long, about the size of a wolf, and a highly active predator. Sprinting on its long muscular hind legs and using its long tail for balance, it could outrun any prey, but it could not fly.

▲ ALXASAURUS

One of the oddest-looking feathered theropods, *Alxasaurus* was 13 ft (4 m) long. Fossilized skin impressions show body coverings of downy feathers, and arms with longer feathers, but these big, slow-moving plant-eaters never got airborne. The colors shown here are guesswork. As with skin, fossil feathers almost never preserve pigments, so scientists can only guess at plumage patterns, based on today's animals.

ARCHAEOPTERYX

One of the world's most famous fossils, the flattened remains of *Archaeopteryx* were first found near Solnhofen, Germany, in limestone strata from the Late Jurassic Period. At first, a single carbonized feather was found in 1859, and then the wonderfully well preserved skeleton of a small, crow-sized animal was discovered. Its long, bony tail and long, thin arms and legs were surrounded by faint but distinct impressions left by long, asymmetrical feathers. These fossil remains were quickly hailed as those of the oldest known bird and given the name *Archaeopteryx*, meaning "ancient wing."

▼ WIDE WINGS

Long arm bones gave *Archaeopteryx* a broad wingspan of around 23 in (58 cm). But it is still unclear whether it could actively fly by flapping its wings, or only glide from tree to tree. Weak flight muscles and a long, bony tail would have made it a clumsy flier. Each arm had three clawed fingers that were probably used for climbing and clinging onto branches.

▲ A CLOSE RELATIVE

Just 12 in (30 cm) long, *Archaeopteryx* was very similar to the small bipedal theropods, especially dromaeosaurs such as *Compsognathus*, above. These were common dinosaurs in the Mid to Late Jurassic Period and are now known to have been feathered but flightless.

◄ MORE MODERN BIRDS

Even if *Archaeopteryx* did fly, it was a very primitive bird. The long bony tail, clawed fingers, and teeth made it very like the small theropods from which it evolved. When the first modern birds evolved, such as this Late Cretaceous seabird, *Ichthyornis*, they still retained primitive toothed jaws. But the long bony tail and clawed wing fingers had gone.

▲ EVIDENCE FOR EVOLUTION

The first fossil feather found for *Archaeopteryx* was clearly asymmetrical, like the flight feathers of modern birds. When a fossil skeleton was found, UK scientist Thomas Henry Huxley pointed out the mixture of reptilian and birdlike features. He was convinced that the feathered *Archaeopteryx* was the link between dinosaurs and birds and proof of Charles Darwin's new Theory of Evolution.

◀ OLDEST KNOWN BIRD

Although *Archaeopteryx* has some dinosaur features, such as clawed fingers, it is generally recognized as the earliest and most primitive bird. Scientists, however, are still searching for the missing link between *Archaeopteryx*, which dates from the Late Jurassic Period about 150 mya, and the modern birds that first emerged in the Late Cretaceous Period.

DETAILED FOSSIL ▶

There are now 11 known specimens of *Archaeopteryx*. The first specimen to be recognized as a bird was found in 1861 and bought by the British Museum in London, but most of the skull is missing. The more complete specimen shown here was found in 1874 and belongs to the Humboldt Museum in Berlin, Germany.

INSIDE A DINOSAUR

To figure out how dinosaurs functioned, scientists need to understand their anatomy—not just their skeletons and teeth but also their muscles and internal organs. They do this mainly through comparisons with dinosaurs' closest living relatives, the birds and crocodiles. Sometimes dinosaur fossils offer clues, too, such as scars on bones showing where muscles were attached, but fossils of the actual muscles and other soft tissue are very rare.

Thick, walled arteries carried blood all the way up to the head

Huge intestines may have held food for a long time while breaking it down

Large gizzard in front of stomach aided digestion

◀ INSIDE A PLANT-EATER

Most plants provide little energy unless eaten in bulk. Big plant-eaters need a big stomach to hold all the food required to fuel the rest of the body. The giant sauropod *Brachiosaurus* was as heavy as 12 elephants and needed to eat 440 lb (200 kg) of leaves a day. But plant fibers are difficult to digest, and since *Brachiosaurus* did not chew its food, it had to rely on digestive juices and microbes in its huge stomach and intestines to help break food down.

▶ INSIDE A MEAT-EATER

Meat provides more energy than plants, so meat-eaters do not need large stomachs and do not need to spend most of their time eating, as plant-eaters do. However, large carnivores, such as this *Carnotaurus*, spent a lot of time and energy hunting and scavenging for food. They needed large lungs to supply oxygen to the bloodstream and a large heart to pump blood quickly to the brain and around the body.

Stomach

Large heart and lungs supplied the high levels of oxygen needed in active hunting

Intestines

Large shoulder and arm muscles powered the long, clawed forelimbs

Ilio-tibial muscle pulled the leg back

▼ EXTRA DIGESTION

Many birds, reptiles, and plant-eating dinosaurs have a special chamber called a gizzard. Its muscular walls churned the food before it was returned to the stomach for further processing by microbes. *Euoplocephalus* was 20 ft (6 m) long and built like a tank, but this low-browsing plant-eater with small teeth could only mash its food, not chew it. So the plant-matter was digested first in the gizzard, then in the large stomach.

Gizzard may have contained gastroliths—small stones that helped grind plant matter

Large stomach

▲ MUSCLES

The bones of the skeleton preserve scars on their surface where muscles and tendons were attached. By studying the position of these scars, scientists can reconstruct the animal's muscles and get some idea of how it moved and behaved. For instance, *Oviraptor* was a small birdlike dinosaur, 6½ ft (2 m) long and lightly built. Its two long legs were powered by special birdlike muscles that allowed it to run fast.

▼ DINOSAUR DROPPINGS

Food passing through an animal's intestines produces waste as dung, or feces. Coprolites are fossilized droppings, and they reveal fascinating details about diet. It is hard to match a coprolite to the species that produced it, but expert analysis of what the coprolite contains can show the different foods digested by plant- and meat-eaters. The coprolites of herbivorous dinosaurs contain seeds, pollen, and occasionally fragments of recognizable leaves. Carnivorous dinosaurs produced coprolites full of bone fragments that can help to identify which animals were hunted.

Most dinosaurs, like today's reptiles, had small brains compared with their body size. In some plant-eating dinosaurs, the brain was very small indeed. However, with the evolution of birdlike theropod dinosaurs, brain size increased relative to body size. Larger brains are required for better coordination between the senses and movement. The theropods' superior brainpower was directly linked to their lifestyle as alert, highly active, and speedy predators, with sharp eyesight used for spotting their next meal.

▼ KENTROSAURUS BRAIN

Even by dinosaur standards, *Kentrosaurus* had a small brain. Although this stegosaur had a bulky body, its skull was small and mostly made up of a long snout and jaw. The space housing the brain, called the cranial cavity, was only the size of a walnut. However, *Kentrosaurus's* brain size does not fall below the average range of reptile brains when measured relative to body weight.

Fossil brain is a cast, formed inside the cranial cavity

Walnut

▼ KENTROSAURUS

Although *Kentrosaurus* grew to 16 ft (5 m) in length, this plant-eater's skull was relatively small and its brain was no larger than a walnut. Scientists used to think that *Kentrosaurus* had a second, larger "brain" at the other end of the spinal cord, which links the brain to the rest of the body's nervous system. However, they now think this back-end brain is more likely to have been an energy store for the nervous system, as in present-day birds.

Hip region where "rear brain" was located

Small skull houses a small brain, just 1 in (2.5 cm) long

▲ TYRANNOSAURUS

Although *Tyrannosaurus rex* had a huge skull 5 ft (1.5 m) long, this theropod's brain cast is just 9 in (23 cm) long. But even that is large compared with most other dinosaurs, and closer to the relative proportions found in birds. The brain cast also has enlarged olfactory bulbs, which relayed information about smell from the nose to the brain, so this predator's sense of smell must have been particularly strong.

Skull shape made brain shorter than usual

Small brain is still three times larger than expected for a reptile of this size

▲ BAROSAURUS

Enormous plant-eating sauropods, such as *Barosaurus*, moved slowly and had brains that, relative to body size, were smaller than the brain of any living reptile. *Barosaurus* was 92 ft (28 m) long. Its small skull had a long snout and behind that was a short cranial cavity that housed a brain merely 5 in (12 cm) long.

Human brain is 5 in (12 cm) wide

Tyrannosaurus rex brain cast

TROODON

Quick-witted and fast on its feet, this small dinosaur had possibly the largest brain of any dinosaur relative to its body size. A light build made this feathered theropod an agile predator, capable of hunting down small, fast-moving prey. Its narrow skull had large, forward-pointing eyes that could accurately judge the distance of its prey before pouncing for the kill, even in dim light at dusk. Its jaws were armed with about 120 small, sharp, inwardly curving, and coarsely serrated teeth. Their shape suggests that, although *Troodon* was primarily a meat-eating predator, it may have also consumed some plant matter and lived as an omnivore.

▼ BIPEDAL SPRINTER

Troodon walked on its long, slender hind legs. The lower leg bones were longer than the upper leg bones, which made these hind limbs well suited to running fast. Each leg ended in long metatarsal foot bones, with three clawed toes. The second toe had a large, sickle-shaped claw, which *Troodon* may have used for pinning down prey. This lethally sharp weapon could swivel upward to stay off the ground and avoid being blunted while *Troodon* was running.

Long lower leg bones

Large claw on second toe

▲ A SKELETON BUILT FOR SPEED

Arms outstretched and jaws open, this mounted skeleton shows *Troodon* as if it is about to pounce on its next victim. Although it was the length of a tall human, *Troodon* was only as heavy as a child. What it lacked in size and power, it made up for with speed. It belonged to the group of dinosaurs called dromaeosaurs ("running lizards"), which are also known as raptors ("thieves"). It is easy to see why.

◀ 3-D VISION

The skull's shape and the position of *Troodon*'s eyes gave it a hunter's forward-looking field of view, covered by both eyes. Images from each eye were merged in its brain to produce a 3-D image and excellent depth perception. As a result, *Troodon*—like many predators today—could focus on its target and accurately judge its distance. This depth perception is important for an active hunter that had to make sudden forward lunges to grab its prey.

▼ BALANCING ACT

Like so many bipedal theropods, *Troodon* had a long tail, which made up about half the animal's length. The tail vertebrae carried small bony, downward-pointing spurs, to which muscles and tendons were attached. This gave strength and rigidity to the tail, which acted as a counterbalance to the rest of the body as *Troodon* raced after its prey.

▼ TROODON'S EGG AND EMBRYO

Numerous fossilized *Troodon* eggs have been found at Egg Mountain in Montana. At this Late Cretaceous nesting site, fossils of adult *Troodon* have been found on top of clutches with an average of 24 eggs. This suggests that the parents sat on their nests to keep the eggs warm and safe, like brooding hens waiting for their eggs to hatch.

RUNNING AND WALKING

Dinosaur footprints and trackways left in soft sand or mud are common trace fossils (see page 34). Since bones are rarely found with the tracks, scientists cannot tell exactly which species made them. But the size and shape of the footprints show roughly what kind of dinosaur it was. Tracks can also capture unique information about dinosaurs' behavior—whether they moved on two legs or four, on their own or in herds, and how fast they could walk or run. Tracks may even record dinosaurs being ambushed by a predator whose distinctive footprints ran into theirs.

❶ EARLIEST REPTILE TRACKS

Fossil trackways of the first vertebrates (backboned animals) on land have been found in rock strata dating back to the Late Devonian Period, 370 million years ago. However, fossil footprints only become common in the following Carboniferous Period, when the first reptiles evolved. These early land-dwelling reptiles remained close to water and left their tracks in swampy forest mud. The five-toed reptile tracks shown here were found in Canada in 2010.

Parallel tracks show dinosaurs moving side by side in pairs or in herds

Deep tracks show that this dinosaur was heavy

❷ THEROPOD TRACKS

Fossil trackways of large, three-toed footprints were first discovered in the 1840s. Scientists realized they had been made by two-legged animals, which they imagined must have been giant birds. However, footprints like these ones from Spain, which are nearly 3¼ ft (1 m) apart, are now known to have been formed by large theropod dinosaurs. Fossil skeletons show that the theropods were bipedal and had birdlike feet with three toes.

❸ LAKESIDE LIFE

Sucre quarry in Bolivia is the largest site of dinosaur tracks, with more than 250 trackways impressed into limestone while it was still soft mud. The original site was a Late Cretaceous lakeside, where various ankylosaurs and giant titanosaurs lumbered along on all fours, and bipedal theropods sprinted after prey. Their tracks were buried, the mud turned to rock, and the rock layer was later tilted up on its side by movements in Earth's crust.

❹ FASTEST RUNNER

Most dinosaur trackways were made by slow-moving quadrupeds, walking at speeds between 2 mph (3 kph) and 9 mph (14.5 kph). Small bipedal dinosaurs, such as the dromaeosaurs, were faster. Some may have hit top speeds of up to 25 mph (40 kph)—as fast as a racehorse. But *Sinornithosaurus* was an exception. This tiny, tree-dwelling dromaeosaur would have been slowed down by the long feathers on its legs.

❺ EXPERT ANALYSIS

The positions of left and right footprints one after another show whether a dinosaur was walking or running. By measuring the spacing between the footprints, known as the stride length, and checking the leg length of different kinds of dinosaurs, scientists can also work out roughly how fast the animal was moving. The tracks of a bipedal theropod such as a big tyrannosaur show how its stride changed as it increased its speed.

Long feathers on limbs were better for gliding than running

Long feathers would get in the way and create too much drag for running

Walking
Stride length 8¾ ft (2.7 m)
Speed 4¼ mph (6.8 kph)

Running
Stride length 18¾ ft (5.7 m)
Speed 18 mph (29.2 kph)

SWIMMING

The marine (sea-dwelling) reptiles that dominated Mesozoic oceans can be linked all the way back to the first vertebrates (backboned animals), which were fish. Some evolved limbs and lungs to leave the water and live on dry land. These land-dwelling, egg-laying animals evolved eventually into reptiles and mammals. But some groups evolved once again into aquatic creatures. These included the now-extinct ichthyosaurs and mosasaurs, and some survivors—turtles and marine mammals, such as whales.

Legs had webbed feet

Flattened tail helped *Acanthostega* to swim

❶ ACANTHOSTEGA
The first four-legged vertebrates were animals such as *Acanthostega*, which was 3¼ ft (1 m) long and lived 365 million years ago. Still primarily aquatic, these vertebrates used their flat tails for swimming. Later, their relatives evolved legs strong enough to walk on land.

❷ PLIOPLATECARPUS
At the end of the dinosaur age, large mosasaurs, such as *Plioplatecarpus*, were some of the fiercest predators in the oceans. Descended from land-dwelling lizards, they were well adapted to fast swimming and could not return to land, but they had to surface for air between dives.

❸ ARCHELON
The giant, Late Cretaceous turtle *Archelon* grew to 13 ft (4 m) long, twice the size of any present-day turtle. It used its four winglike paddles to "fly" through the water, but it had to return to dry land to lay its eggs—as turtles still do today.

Neck was half the total
body length of 30 ft (9 m)

Long, narrow
snout with rows
of sharp teeth

❹ ELASMOSAURUS
The plesiosaurs, such as the giant *Elasmosaurus*, terrorized Jurassic and Cretaceous oceans. With streamlined bodies, flipperlike limbs, and ferocious fangs, they were well adapted to life as marine predators but were themselves attacked by other predators.

❺ TEMNODONTOSAURUS
Predatory ichthyosaurs, such as the 40-ft-(12-m-) long *Temnodontosaurus*, formed a group of reptiles that were totally independent of the land. They gave birth to live young at sea, but came to the surface to breathe. With dolphinlike bodies, they were fast hunters of fish and squid.

❻ NOTHOSAURUS
The nothosaurs, which included *Nothosaurus*, were reptiles that returned to the sea in the Triassic Period. These fish-hunters were good swimmers, with streamlined bodies and webbed feet; some also had claws. They probably clambered ashore to rest and breed.

❼ KRONOSAURUS
In addition to the long-necked forms, such as *Elasmosaurus*, the plesiosaurs evolved into short-necked forms called pliosaurs, such as the Late Cretaceous *Kronosaurus*. This predator grew to 30 ft (9 m) and was one of the largest marine reptiles. Its massive skull was 10 ft (3 m) long.

ICHTHYOSAURUS

At first glance, *Ichthyosaurus* looks like a dolphin. It was actually a marine reptile and typical of the Mesozoic ichthyosaurs that evolved from earlier land-dwelling reptiles. *Ichthyosaurus* had the streamlined, muscular body and tail of a fast hunter. Using its large eyes to detect prey, it shot into a school of fish like a torpedo and snatched its victims as they scattered. Its long, pointed beak was lined with rows of sharp teeth, and its fossilized stomach contents reveal a varied diet of fish, squid, and other mollusks.

Fossilized remains of the ichthyosaur *Stenopterygius* and its young

▼ SEA-DWELLING REPTILE

Ichthyosaurus hunted in the shallow seas of Early Jurassic Europe, about 190 mya. It was 6½ ft (2 m) long, with nostrils at the top of its beak, close to its eyes, and it surfaced to breathe between dives.

BUILT FOR SWIMMING ▶

Fossilized remains show that ichthyosaurs had powerful shoulders and limbs shaped like flippers. The end of the spine bent downward to support the large tail fin, which beat from side to side to power the animal through the water like a shark.

◀ REPRODUCTION

Most reptiles today lay eggs on land. However, the ichthyosaurs became so well-adapted to marine life that they evolved the ability to retain the developing embryo in the female's body and gave birth to live and fully independent young. Dolphins and some sharks do the same.

▶ MASSIVE EYES

The ichthyosaur skull had very large eye sockets, surrounded by a ring of small bones. These provided support for the enormous eyes, which allowed ichthyosaurs to see their prey even in the low light levels of deep or murky waters.

FLYING

Prehistoric life took to the air more than 300 million years ago, when insects were the first group of animal to develop wings and master the ability to fly. They were followed by flying reptiles, then birds, and then mammals. Flight not only gave these groups the means to escape from enemies on the ground but also helped them to search more quickly for food, mates, and shelter over a wider area. Flying animals could also spread more widely, crossing spans of water to reach more distant lands and migrate from the best feeding grounds to the best places for breeding.

Long, bony tail

◄ EARLY BAT
Bats are the only mammals capable of flapping flight. Their wings are formed of a thin, leathery membrane of skin stretched across several long fingers. One of the earliest bats, *Icaronycteris* flew 50 mya.

EARLY BIRD ▼
Iberomesornis was a fully feathered, sparrow-sized, insect-chasing bird from the Early Cretaceous Period. Unlike *Archaeopteryx* and other primitive birds in the Late Jurassic Period, *Iberomesornis* had large chest bones that show it was capable of flapping flight. Its curved foot claws suggest that it could also perch on trees like present-day birds.

Extra-long finger bone

▼ DRAGONFLIES
Insects took flight in the Carboniferous Period, 359–299 mya. Dragonflies are among the oldest and most successful groups still living and included the large, Jurassic *Libellulium*, which had a wingspan of nearly 6 in (14 cm). Today's dragonflies are among the world's fastest insects, and they can fly in any direction—even backward—as they flit over ponds and streams in search of prey and places to breed.

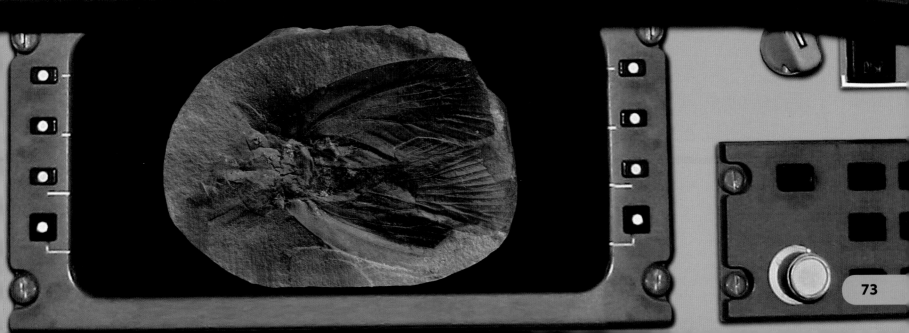

▼ EUDIMORPHODON

The reptilian pterosaurs were the first successful and diverse group of flying vertebrate. Their wings were made of a featherless membrane of leathery skin stretching from the body and legs to the arm bones and a very long fourth finger. Late Triassic *Eudimorphodon* was one of the earliest pterosaurs to take to the skies.

Body and wings covered in hairy fuzz

▼ COCKROACH

Archimylacris was a cockroachlike insect called a blattopteran. Among the earliest flying insects, the blattopterans lived in the swampy forests of the Carboniferous Period, about 300 mya. They had two pairs of wings that folded back over their bodies, with the toughened front wings covering the more delicate hind wings. Some blattopterans grew to 2 in (5 cm) long.

Sharp pointed teeth grasped slippery fish

PTERODACTYLUS

The pterosaurs dominated the skies above the dinosaurs. Although some had huge wingspans the size of a small airplane, *Pterodactylus* (meaning "winged finger") was more like a stork or a heron. It was originally mistaken for a sea creature with flippers, or a mammal with wings like a bat. But in 1809, it became the first animal to be correctly identified as a flying reptile. Many complete skeletons have been found, mostly in the Late Jurassic limestone strata of Solnhofen in southern Germany. *Pterodactylus* is now the best-known pterosaur of all.

▼ WHITE PELICAN

Some of today's large, fish-eating birds show how *Pterodactylus* may have hunted for prey. Soaring through the air on long wings, some pelicans fly more than 60 miles (100 km) a day in search of fish, crustaceans, turtles, and chicks, which they scoop up in their long beaks. They fish alone and in groups, swimming and diving, and even snatch prey from other birds.

Long bill scoops up prey from the water—or from other birds

▶ FLYING HIGH

Pterodactylus flew over coastal waters, snatching small fish. Exactly how it took off, flew, landed, and walked is still debated. Some pterosaurs had tails, which may have helped them to steer through the air, but others were tail-less. Most had bony head crests, which may also have been used for steering, or for display.

Pterodactylus depicted in flight

▶ IMAGINING THE PAST

By 1830, pterosaurs such as *Pterodactylus* were portrayed as batlike flying reptiles. "Duria Antiquor—a more Ancient Dorset," painted by the English geologist Henry De la Beche, was the first attempt to reconstruct a prehistoric scene from what was then known about the Jurassic fossils of Dorset, England, especially those found by English fossil-hunter Mary Anning.

▲ WINGS

Preserved traces of soft tissue tell us a lot about pterosaurs' wings. The leathery membrane had thin layers of muscle and blood vessels, all stiffened and reinforced by layers of hairlike fibers. The membrane was strong enough to provide lift for takeoff and flight, but flexible enough to be folded when the animal landed.

▲ FLYING FOX

The largest bats today are the fruit bats, also known as flying foxes. They are similar in size to *Pterodactylus* and, like all bats, have a similar wing structure, with skin stretched between the arms, long finger bones, and legs. For bats and pterosaurs alike, the body was covered in fur.

▲ LONG NECK

Pterodactylus was one of the smallest of the pterosaurs, but it had a longer neck and shorter tail than earlier pterosaurs, making it much more agile in flight. It is one of more than 100 species of pterosaur, which first evolved in the Late Triassic Period, probably from the reptiles that also gave rise to the dinosaurs.

▶ FOSSIL SKELETON

Complete skeletons of *Pterodactylus* show typical pterosaur features. With skin stretched over the long fourth finger, this animal had a wingspan of up to 4 ft (1.2 m), while the short tail gave a body length of no more than 1 ft (30 cm). The skull's long, narrow jaws had a hooked tip and sharp, pointed teeth.

REPRODUCTION

As reptiles, every dinosaur began life in an egg that was fertilized inside its mother's body. When the egg was laid, it contained enough nutrients for its embryo to continue to grow and then hatch from the shell. Dinosaurs scraped mounds or hollows for nests and laid clutches of up to 40 eggs. Some dinosaurs stayed to protect their eggs and feed their hatchlings. Larger species may have covered them with vegetation and left them to fend for themselves.

Arms, which were probably feathered, spread over the eggs to protect them

▶ EGG WITH EMBRYO

Although some dinosaurs were enormous, their eggs were never more than 2 ft (60 cm) long. Any larger, and the shell would have been too thick for the hatchling to break. This egg is from a fossilized nest in Mongolia's Gobi Desert. Just 7 in (18 cm) long, it contains the embryo of an *Oviraptor*. Fossilized embryos are extremely fragile and rare, but their tiny bones help scientists figure out which dinosaur laid the eggs.

Embryo of Late Cretaceous *Oviraptor*

▲ FROM EMBRYO TO GIANT

The tiny crushed embryo of a Cretaceous titanosaur is preserved in this fossil egg from Argentina. About 5½ in (14 cm) long, it is one of thousands of titanosaur eggs found in the area. These giant plant-eaters probably lived in herds and nested together.

▶ GUARDING THE EGGS

Like *Oviraptor*, *Citipati* was another Late Cretaceous oviraptorosaur from Mongolia. Found in 1995, this amazing fossil vividly preserves an adult *Citipati* that died while sitting on top of a clutch of eggs. She was brooding her eggs like a hen, keeping them warm and safe. The clutch contained more than 20 large, oval eggs, each up to 7 in (18 cm) long. The eggs were arranged in circular layers.

▲ MAIASAURA NEST

Numerous nest hollows with fossilized eggs and hatchlings have been found at Egg Mountain in Montana. Some eggs still contain the bones of embryos. They belong to the hadrosaur *Maiasaura*, whose name means "good mother." At this Late Cretaceous nesting site, many females repeatedly returned to lay their eggs. The presence of juveniles at the site suggests that adults stayed to look after them.

Adult *Maiasaura* feeding its young and guarding its new hatchlings

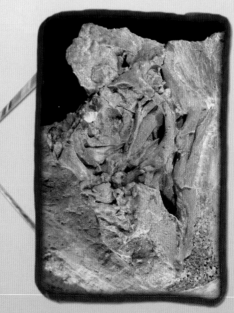

▶A CLUTCH OF EGGS

The name *Oviraptor* means "egg thief." This egg cluster was discovered in Mongolia's Gobi Desert in the 1920s, with the remains of a small, bipedal dinosaur. The dinosaur was thought to have died while trying to steal the eggs from a ceratopsian nest. However, it is now known from further finds that the nest was hers. She was guarding the eggs, not stealing them.

Long, oval eggs, laid 75 million years ago

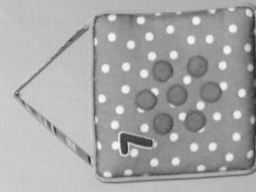

TEMPERATURE CONTROL

Scientists used to think that dinosaurs were cold-blooded, as most reptiles are. Reptiles' body temperatures depend on their surroundings. When it is cold, their bodies are cold and they are sluggish. Only when the Sun warms them up can they become active. But the study of dinosaur bones shows that many dinosaurs grew fast and were highly active, like birds and mammals, which are warm-blooded. Being warm-blooded means that their internal metabolism—the chemical processes that generate energy—maintains a high, constant body temperature and a more active lifestyle.

❶ GIGANTOTHERMS

Even if they were cold-blooded, sauropods, such as this 39-ft- (12-m-) long *Saltasaurus,* were so large that their bodies took a long time to heat up or cool down. In fact, their core temperature may not have varied with their surroundings at all. Even cold-blooded animals generate some metabolic heat, so sauropods may have maintained a high body temperature by being "gigantothermic"—meaning they were so large their temperature stayed the same.

❶

Sail fin was possibly used for regulating body heat but also in display

❷ RADIATING SAIL

The theropods were by and large highly active predators. This Early Cretaceous theropod was a spinosaur, with tall spines on its backbone forming a large fin like a sail. The sail increased the animal's skin area and may have been used for thermoregulation—controlling the body temperature. With blood vessels running through the sail, the animal could take in more heat by basking in the Sun, or shed heat like a radiator by standing in the shade.

Huge size helped retain body heat, as it does in elephants and large sharks

❸ DOWNY COAT

Famous for its vicious claws and teeth, this long-legged theropod was a fast-running meat-eater. Growing to no more than 10 ft (3 m) long, *Deinonychus* would have had to maintain a high body temperature to remain active and may have been warm-blooded. As a dromaeosaurid, it was probably feathered, which would have helped insulate the body and prevent heat loss.

❹ POLAR DINOSAUR

Leaellynasaura was a small, 3¼-ft- (1-m-) long ornithopod from Early Cretaceous Australia and one of several dinosaurs found in polar latitudes, where cold-blooded reptiles do not normally survive. Even though there were no polar ice sheets, the winter nights were long, dark, and decidedly cool. These dinosaurs must have been relatively warm-blooded, with some internal thermoregulation, to have survived in polar regions.

❺ ANTARCTIC GIANT

The largest Early Jurassic theropod was also the largest predator among several dinosaurs now known from Antarctica. *Cryolophosaurus* grew to about 23 ft (7 m) long and weighed more than 1,000 lb (450 kg), and it had a strange, bony crest on top of its skull. Although this dinosaur had no evident adaptations for temperature control, it could somehow survive the long, dark winters of the Antarctic.

Cryolophosaurus means "cold crest lizard"

Downy covering insulated the body

STEGOSAURUS

The stegosaurs formed an eye-catching group of heavily built plant-eating dinosaurs that had two rows of massive, bony plates along the back, running from neck to tail. Stegosaurs also had large, bony spikes at the end of the tail. Typical of this group was the Late Jurassic *Stegosaurus*, from North America, which grew to 33 ft (10 m) long and weighed more than 2 tons. This animal must have consumed vast amounts of vegetation.

❹ HIP BONES

The bony structure of *Stegosaurus*'s hip was typically ornithischian, with the pubic bone pointing backward. The hip bones were massively built and heavily muscled to connect with the powerful hind legs and carry much of the body's considerable weight.

❸ PUZZLING PLATES

The most striking feature of *Stegosaurus* is the series of bony plates that were attached to its back. Scientists have long debated their purpose: were they used for protection, or display, or controlling body temperature? Display seems the most likely answer—to impress others in the herd and attract a mate.

❷ TAIL BONES

Nearly half of *Stegosaurus*'s body length was made up of its tail. The tail was probably stiff at the base, but the spiked end may have been quite flexible and could have lashed out at predators.

❶ TAIL SPIKES

Two pairs of sharp bony spikes, up to 3 ft (90 cm) long, were attached to the end of the tail. Some scientists think these spikes were probably protective—maybe *Stegosaurus* swung its tail in self-defense against predators. But the spikes may also have been used for display.

❺ LEGS

The strong, muscled hind legs of this quadruped (an animal walking on all fours) were much longer than the front legs and supported much of the animal's weight. Because of the difference in leg length, the neck and head were held lower than the tops of the hips.

❻ RIB CAGE

The broad rib cage was made of about 16 pairs of stout rib bones that were attached to the backbone and extended downward, protecting the lungs and other body organs. They also provided support for the stegosaur's bulky stomach and intestines.

❼ SHORT NECK

The short neck hung low from the shoulder girdle. The neck carried the first back plates and the small skull, which probably hung no more than 3¼ ft (1 m) above the ground. The neck plates contained blood vessels, so they may have helped to control the animal's body temperature.

❽ SMALL SKULL

The skull was long, narrow, and very small in proportion to the massive body. The long jaws had a toothless beak that cropped low-growing vegetation and small triangular cheek teeth that then chewed it. At the back of the skull, the space for the brain, called the cranial cavity, carried a walnut-sized brain.

❾ FEET

Despite *Stegosaurus*'s heavy weight, its feet were shaped in such a way that the dinosaur stood on its toes, with a supporting pad behind each toe. Each front leg had three toes and each hind leg had five toes, with blunt hooves on the inner two.

KILLER INSTINCTS

Tyrannosaurus rex was one of the largest ever meat-eaters on land and had a bone-crunching bite. It is not entirely clear, however, whether it used its keen sense of smell for active hunting or scavenging, or both.

Senses and behavior

DINOSAUR SENSES

To survive, animals have to sense what is going on in their surroundings. Dinosaurs were no exception. Whether they were plant-eaters in danger of being preyed upon by meat-eaters, or predators in pursuit of their next meal, dinosaurs needed well-developed senses. The fossilized bones of eye sockets, inner ears, and nasal passages contain clues about how the main groups of dinosaurs saw, heard, and smelled the world around them. Together with brain casts (see pages 62–63), these details show significant differences in how their senses developed.

Lambeosaurus's hollow crest may have helped produce trombonelike calls

❶ SMELL
A keen sense of smell is particularly important for some predators, especially if they cannot see their potential prey because they have weak eyesight, if there is not much light, or if the prey is hiding or at a distance. The brain casts of theropod tyrannosaurs and dromaeosaurs, such as this *Utahraptor*, show enlarged olfactory bulbs that relayed detailed information about smell from the nose to the brain.

Ear structure well suited to detecting the deep, booming sounds made by others

❷

Acute sense of smell helped *Utahraptor*, the largest dromaeosaur, to find its victims

❶

❷ HEARING
Animals need ears that are sensitive to the calls used to keep group members in touch and warn of approaching danger. Computed tomography (CT) scans of the skulls of crested hadrosaurs show that the bone structure inside the ear provided good hearing, especially for deep, reverberating sounds. The hadrosaurs' hollow crests may have been used to produce the same kind of sounds. Elephants today make deep, rumbling sounds for long-distance communication.

Forward-pointing eyes provide an overlapping field of view

❸ EYESIGHT

Most dinosaurs' eyes were on each side of the skull, giving a wide view of their surroundings. With little or no overlap between what the left and right eyes could see (their fields of view), these dinosaurs were unable to see things in three dimensions (3-D) and judge how close they were. However, some theropods had forward-facing eyes with overlapping fields of view, which enabled them to see in 3-D and judge the distance to their prey before pouncing. *Carnotaurus* was a large theropod and although its eyes were small, their position on the skull gave this predator 3-D vision.

❹ EXTRA-LARGE EYES

The larger an eye is, the better it is at gathering light from its surroundings and helping an animal to see, even when there is little light. However, large eyes require large eye sockets in the skull. In some dinosaurs, such as the small ceratopsian *Protoceratops*, support and added protection for large eyeballs was provided by an extra ring of bones, known as a sclerotic ring.

Large eyeball supported by ring of bones

COMMUNICATION AND DISPLAY

Like all animals, dinosaurs must have interacted in many ways and for many reasons. Animals living in a group today use calls and visual signals to stay in contact, keep the group together, and warn of any approaching danger. But within these social groups there are tensions between males competing for females and territory. Even solitary males living outside a group have to attract mates and intimidate or fight rival males. Serious conflict can lead to life-threatening injuries, so intimidation through display is also important. Success may depend not just on physical strength but also on having large horns or a flamboyant head crest. All of this must have been true for dinosaurs, too.

▼ EINIOSAURUS

Ceratopsians such as *Einiosaurus* had elaborate neck frills, which may have shielded the back of the neck from predators' teeth and claws. But the frills were not especially strong and so it seems more likely that they were used in display, to attract females and threaten rival males.

▲ PARASAUROLOPHUS

Little is known about dinosaur calls, but *Parasaurolophus* and some of the other hadrosaurs had hollow bony structures, such as long tubular crests, on their skulls. The crest may have been used like a trombone, producing deep rumbling sounds when air was blown from the nostrils through hollow chambers inside the crest.

◄ CORYTHOSAURUS

This large hadrosaur had a rounded bony head crest that was hollow and may have been used to generate loud booming calls. Elephants make low rumbling sounds that travel a considerable distance, even through wooded landscapes. Similar calls could have helped keep a herd of hadrosaurs in contact, especially when the herd was spread out and the animals could not see one another.

◄ CAUDIPTERYX

Well preserved fossils show that *Caudipteryx* had long feathers on its arms and tail, but could not fly, so maybe the feathers were used for display. Fossils rarely preserve color but, as in birds today, perhaps males attracted mates with gaudily colored feathers, while females hid from predators by camouflaging themselves with duller feathers.

◄ PACHYCEPHALOSAURUS

Pachycephalosaurus had an unusually thick, domed skull. Rival males may have charged at each other in head-butting contests, much like wild sheep and goats do today. However, these dinosaurs had curved necks that do not look strong enough to withstand the force of the impact. Perhaps the skull and its surrounding frill of knobby bones were largely used in display. There may still have been some sideways head-butting.

TRICERATOPS

Herds of *Triceratops* must have been an impressive sight in the landscapes of North America in the Late Cretaceous Period. With its massive horned skull, this quadrupedal plant-eating dinosaur was built like a giant rhinoceros. Heavy and slow-moving, it was a tempting target for large predators. But it was well protected by two long brow horns and a shorter nose horn. No wonder this dinosaur was given the name *Triceratops*, meaning "three-horned face."

◀ THREE HORNS, HOW MANY TRICERATOPS?

Numerous fossil specimens have been found and many are complete. Together, they show all the different stages of growth from hatchling to adult. Scientists once thought there were some 15 different species, based on variations in horn shape and size. But most of these are probably just differences between individuals, and so now there are only two known species.

◀ STURDY SKELETON

Growing to 30 ft (9 m) long, *Triceratops* was as heavy as a 10-ton (9-metric ton) truck and had a sturdy skeleton. The massive shoulders and four short but sturdy legs needed powerful muscles for supporting the animal's bulk, especially its long, heavy tail and huge head. The animal's feet ended in hooflike bones.

▼ LARGE NECK FRILL

Triceratops belonged to a group of horned dinosaurs called ceratopsians. They developed a huge fan-shaped frill of bone extending from the back of the skull and over the neck. With a spectacular variety of bony knobs and spikes, these neck frills were used partly for defense but also for display by males to attract mates.

▶ STYRACOSAURUS

Styracosaurus was smaller than *Triceratops*. But it still had an impressively large skull—6 ft (1.8 m) long, with a single nose horn and an array of six spines growing to almost 24 in (60 cm) from the neck frill. Only juveniles had brow horns, which shrank as they grew older.

▶ FACING THE ENEMY

From the parrotlike beak used to graze on plants to the top of the neck frill, the *Triceratops'* skull grew to 6½ ft (2 m) long—one of the largest skulls of any land animal. The two forward-pointing brow horns were 2¼ ft (70 cm) long and could inflict serious damage on any predator or rival male.

PLANT-EATERS

Plants are plentiful and form the base of a food chain in which plant-eaters, or herbivores, are the next link. Plant-eaters are the most common land-dwelling animals and greatly outnumber the carnivores, or meat-eaters, that prey on them. However, plants have developed various defenses against being eaten, from prickly thorns to poisonous juices, and are difficult to digest. Herbivores have had to evolve various aids to reaching and digesting their food, and plant-eating dinosaurs were no exception. Of the 1,000 known species of dinosaur, 65 percent were plant-eaters.

◄ PLATEOSAURUS

The first dinosaurs were small, but over time a group of mainly plant-eating prosauropods grew taller and heavier. *Plateosaurus* was one of the largest prosauropods and grew to about 26 ft (8 m) long. Standing on its powerful hind legs and stretching up with its long neck, it could reach high tree branches and chomp through tough stems and foliage.

► HUAYANGOSAURUS

At 15 ft (4.5 m) long, *Huayangosaurus* was a small stegosaur from China. It had a shorter, broader snout than later stegosaurs and teeth at the front of its upper jaw instead of a horny beak. Stegosaur feeding habits may have evolved from raking foliage with teeth to cropping it with a toothless beak.

▶ BRACHIOSAURUS

This dinosaur was one of the sauropods, the largest creatures ever to walk the Earth. Unable to rear up on its hind legs, it used its long neck and small skull with peglike teeth to browse on treetops 30 ft (9 m) or more above ground—twice the height reached by any giraffe.

▼ IGUANODON

This was the first plant-eating dinosaur to be found, in 1822. The size of an elephant, it walked mainly on all fours and fed on low-growing plants. Its name means "iguana teeth" because its leaf-shaped teeth were similar to those of today's iguanas, although 20 times larger.

◀ PENTACERATOPS

This huge ceratopsian was 23 ft (7 m) long and had one of the largest skulls of any known land animal. Below the spectacular neck frill and horns, the skull narrowed into a hooked, bony snout like a parrot's beak. The beak was used for plucking tough plants, which were then munched by a battery of cheek teeth before being swallowed.

EDMONTOSAURUS

The duck-billed hadrosaurs called *Edmontosaurus* lived on the coastal plains of western North America in the Late Cretaceous Period. About 43 ft (13 m) long, these impressive plant-eaters were the dinosaur equivalents of today's cattle and chewed their way through enormous quantities of plant matter. Despite its size, *Edmontosaurus* was likely preyed upon by tyrannosaurids.

❹

❶ **SKELETON**
The backbone, pelvis, and leg bones of *Edmontosaurus* were strong enough to carry the large stomach of a plant-eater. With its long, muscular tail and large head, it weighed about 4 tons.

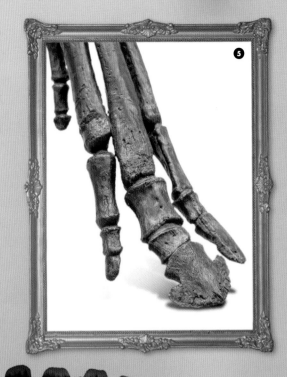

❸ COMMUNICATION
Although this hadrosaur did not have a hollow, sound-making crest on its skull, it did have large hollows around its nostrils. These may have housed balloonlike sacs that produced loud calls when they were inflated.

❹ DUCK-BILLED SKULL
Edmontosaurus's skull widened at the front into a broad "duck-bill" covered with a horny beak. This allowed it to crop large quantities of tough plant material. It would keep food in its cheeks, and chew with the large battery of cheek teeth.

❺ FOUR FINGERS
The slender front limbs ended in long, thin hands. Each had four slender fingers, three of which were tipped with blunt hooves, but no thumb.

❷ STANDING TALL
Normally, *Edmontosaurus* walked on all fours. However, its long, strong hind legs allowed the animal to rear up and reach tall plants. Its heavy tail would stop it from falling over as it did so.

❻ THREE-TOED FEET
Like all hadrosaurs, *Edmontosaurus* stood on powerful rear feet. Each foot had three strong toes tipped with rounded hooves that could support most of the animal's weight.

MEAT-EATERS

Like today's carnivores, meat-eating dinosaurs hunted and killed other animals or scavenged on the remains of animals that were already dead. Meat is a high-protein, high-energy food, so carnivores do not need to eat as much as plant-eaters. But hunting takes a lot of time and energy, and prey can be agile or well defended, so predators had to be quick-witted, strong, and well armed. There weren't that many of them. For every one tyrannosaur, for example, there were four plant-eaters.

Compsognathus had small, sharp teeth used for biting and tearing

◄ COMPSOGNATHUS

Late Jurassic *Compsognathus* was a small theropod, just 3¼ ft (1 m) long. This highly active meat-eater probably had an insulating body-covering of fuzzy feathers. It scavenged and hunted small vertebrates, such as lizards, mammals, and baby dinosaurs, which it caught with its slender but strong arms. Each hand had three robust, clawed fingers.

Like most meat-eaters, *Compsognathus* would scavenge on large carcasses whenever it could

◄ SPINOSAURUS

The largest theropod of all, this giant predator lived along the coast of North Africa during the Cretaceous Period and grew to 52 ft (16 m) long. It had a narrow, crocodile-like skull and straight teeth of various sizes. The teeth suggest that its main diet was fish, but it probably also preyed on any animals it could catch with its muscular arms and three-clawed hands.

Spinosaurus's teeth were straight and conical-shaped, adapted to holding slippery fish

▲ TARBOSAURUS

The giant Asian theropod *Tarbosaurus* was a Late Cretaceous tyrannosaur. With its massive head, powerful jaws, and sharp teeth, it could deliver a bone-crushing bite. It preyed on sauropods, ankylosaurs, and hadrosaurs such as *Barsboldia*, illustrated here. In addition, it probably took any opportunity to scavenge on the kills made by smaller predators.

Velociraptor attacked its prey with its sharp claws

A bony frill protected *Proceratops*'s neck

▶ CARNOTAURUS

The Argentinian theropod *Carnotaurus* was a fast-moving, 30-ft- (9-m-) long predator that lived in the Late Cretaceous Period. It had a powerful neck and a short, deep head. However, its lower jaw and teeth were relatively slender, so *Carnotaurus* probably killed or disabled its prey with a series of fast bites—or scavenged on dead meat.

Long, stiff tail held straight out to balance rest of body

Tiny arms too puny to grapple with prey

Long legs capable of chasing prey at speeds up to 30 mph (50 kph)

▲ MORTAL COMBAT

A fossil showing evidence of a meat-eating theropod dinosaur attacking a plant-eater was found in Late Cretaceous rocks in Mongolia in the 1920s. It shows a predatory *Velociraptor* locked in a deadly duel with a plant-eating *Protoceratops*. The victim had its beak firmly clamped around its attacker's arm when they were both suffocated and buried by a sudden sand storm.

BEAKS, BILLS, AND TEETH

From long, slicing teeth the size of steak knives to rows of stumpy cheek teeth used for grinding leaves, teeth are among the most commonly found fossils. Together with jawbones, beaks, and bills, they reveal a great deal about what kind of food dinosaurs ate and how they caught, gripped, and sometimes chewed it before swallowing. Plant-eaters had to crop and grind pieces of foliage, while meat-eaters quickly tore off chunks of flesh, with little chewing before swallowing and digestion.

❶ BARYONYX

This fish-eater had a crocodile-like skull with 96 pointed teeth lining its long, narrow, curving jaws. Its nostrils were high up the snout so it could breathe while plunging its jaws under water, and its teeth meshed together to grip slippery fish.

❸ TYRANNOSAURUS REX

Armed with up to 58 long, sharp teeth, Tyrannosaurus's massive jaws delivered a powerful bite. Curved like daggers and serrated like steak knives, these teeth could slice into hide, flesh, and bone. They were replaced throughout the dinosaur's life.

❷ PSITTACOSAURUS

Psittacosaurus had a short, deep skull narrowing into a toothless beak like that of a parrot. The beak was used for stripping plant foliage. Teeth used for chewing the food lined the cheeks.

❹ STEGOSAURUS

Instead of front teeth, *Stegosaurus* had a horny beak used for cropping vegetation before chomping it into a pulp between rows of small, leaf-shaped cheek teeth.

❺ EDMONTOSAURUS

Edmontosaurus had a broad, toothless, ducklike bill at the front of its mouth and multiple rows of tiny teeth at the back, which ground down the tough plant food and were continually replaced.

Tyrannosaurus rex tooth

Stegosaurus tooth

Edmontosaurus tooth

⑥ ALLOSAURUS

Allosaurus was another giant, tyrannosaur-like meat-eater with a massive skull. Its jaws could open wide to deliver large slashing bites with long bladelike teeth. By continuously replacing its teeth, this dinosaur kept its deadly bite throughout its life.

QUETZALCOATLUS

One of the most impressive sights in the skies of Cretaceous times would have been the giant pterosaurs, such as *Quetzalcoatlus* and *Ornithocheirus*. With wingspans of about 33 ft (10 m)—the size of a World War II fighter plane—these were the largest animals ever to have taken to the air. Lacking feathers, their wings were made of a thin membrane of skin stretching from their wrists to their ankles.

◀ LONG BEAK

Quetzalcoatlus belonged to a group of pterosaurs known as the azdarchids, which had extremely long necks, large heads, and long, spearlike, toothless beaks. The enormous beak of *Quetzalcoatlus* grew up to 8 ft (2.5 m) long.

◀ QUETZALCOATLUS

This long-necked pterosaur lived in Late Cretaceous America and is named after an Aztec serpent god. Its wingspan reached up to 39 ft (12 m) long. Despite its size, its weight was limited to about 550 lb (250 kg) by an extensive system of air sacs in its bones, meaning that it weighed less than a man-made flying machine of similar size. It is thought to have fed by stalking small animals on land.

ORNITHOCHEIRUS ▶

Early Cretaceous *Ornithocheirus* was another giant pterosaur, with an estimated wingspan of 33 ft (10 m). Like *Quetzalcoatlus*, it is only known from fragments, and its body form is not known. Reconstructions of *Ornithocheirus* are based on fossils of a better-known but smaller relative from South America called *Anhanguera*.

▼ FOLDABLE WINGS
Quetzalcoatlus probably folded its wingtips up and out of the way when foraging on the ground. With its wings folded, it could place the knuckle and its three short fingers on the ground so that it could walk on all fours.

▲ BUILT TO FLY
The pterosaur wing had a very special construction. The short upper arm bones brought the elbow close to the body, while the lower arm bones were much longer. The wing was extended even farther by an enormously long fourth finger, itself made of a series of four long bones.

Long fourth finger

OFFENSIVE WEAPONS

Claws and teeth were among the first offensive weapons evolved by predators more than 500 mya. They were used not only for attack—for capturing and killing prey—but also for fighting between rival males. Meat-eaters used their teeth for disabling or killing prey and tearing off pieces of flesh. Many also had long claws that they used to grab, stab, and hold the carcass while feeding. Although some plant-eaters, too, had claws, theirs were mostly defensive, and were used for fighting off predators.

◀ SCISSOR HANDS

Therizinosaurus was an unusual theropod that probably ate plants. This bipedal dinosaur had arms that were 6½ ft (2 m) long, ending in three fingers with vicious claws nearly 3¼ ft (1 m) long—handy for lashing out in self-defense.

Sickle-shaped claw

▶ TOE CLAWS

Dromaeosaurus, *Deinonychus*, and *Velociraptor* were small but dangerous. These bipedal theropods were dromaeosaurs, known for speed and an extra-large, sickle-shaped claw on their second toe. They could swivel the toe upward when running, to keep from blunting the claw on the ground, and then slash it downward into their prey.

▲ CLAWED HANDS

Spinosaurs, such as this *Irritator*, were large, fish-eating theropods with long, crocodile-like jaws and teeth. They also had large, curving claws on their fingers, which were probably used for hooking slippery fish from the water. No doubt, the claws and fearsome jaws were also used by males sparring over females.

▲ TEETH FOR SLICING

The teeth of meat-eating dinosaurs have evolved different shapes suited to different purposes. Sharply pointed conical teeth are used for piercing and holding a victim's flesh. Slightly backward-curving and blade-shaped teeth with serrated edges are more effective for slicing it. It was these blade-shaped teeth that lined *Allosaurus*'s powerful jaws.

TYRANNOSAURUS REX

Tyrannosaurus rex is the most famous of all dinosaurs. It is often considered the most dangerous and ferocious animal that has ever lived. However, we now know there were even larger meat-eating dinosaurs, such as *Spinosaurus* (see page 94). Even so, *Tyrannosaurus* is still the best known of the giant meat-eaters, thanks to the discovery of some nearly complete specimens. It is a member of a group of large carnivores known as the tyrannosaurids.

Jaws could give a
bone-crunching bite

▶ HUNTER OR SCAVENGER?

Was *Tyrannosaurus* a predator or a scavenger? Its arms were too small to hold prey, and its highly developed sense of smell was perfect for sniffing out rotting carcasses. In addition, its bone-crushing bite allowed it to chew on the bone marrow of dead bodies, and bone fragments found in its droppings support the idea that it was a scavenger. However, its predatory features included binocular vision, which hunters use to judge distance. It was a fast mover, too—ideal for hunting. Fossils have been found with healed wounds, which were probably caused by fighting. Evidence shows that it was most likely both a hunter and a scavenger.

Tiny hand had
only two fingers

▼ BALANCING ACT

Tyrannosaurus grew to 40 ft (12 m) in length and weighed about 5 tons. Its stiffly muscular tail was about 16 ft (5 m) long. Its body and tail were balanced on its hips, about 13 ft (4 m) above the ground.

Long, stiff, muscular tail used for balance

Strong, birdlike feet and toes

◄ CLAWED FINGERS

Tyrannosaurus had unusually small arms, no more than 3¼ ft (1 m) long. Its hands, which had just two clawed fingers, could not reach its mouth. However, the arms were still very muscular. They must have had a particular job to do, but scientists are not entirely sure what that was. Perhaps the arms helped a sitting *Tyrannosaurus* to rise up from the ground.

Holes reduce skull weight

MASSIVE SKULL ►

Tyrannosaurus had a huge head, which was 5 ft (1.5 m) long. The skull's weight was reduced by a scaffolding-like bony structure with large holes. Massive muscles passed through the holes. Its long jaws could deliver an immensely powerful bite. It had 58 serrated, bladelike teeth—with 6 in (15 cm) exposed above the gums—that it used to pierce skin, flesh, and even bone. The narrow snout gave the eyes an overlapping field of view, which allowed binocular vision—the ability to judge distance accurately before lunging at prey.

Deep, strong jawbone

Serrated, flesh-cutting teeth

DEFENSIVE WEAPONS

Plant-eating dinosaurs had two main methods of defending themselves against meat-eating predators—running away or standing and fighting. Large, slow-moving plant-eaters had to stand and fight and, therefore, evolved a variety of defensive structures. Some of these, such as head horns, thumb spikes, and tail clubs, were weapons, while body spines and plates were defensive body armor.

Iguanodon's thumb spike was its only weapon against an attacker

Sharp brow horns were an effective deterrent

Cheek spikes protected the side of the face

▲ THUMB SPIKES

Some plant-eaters, such as *Iguanodon*, had few defensive weapons. They depended on their size and herd behavior to protect them from predators. However, *Iguanodon* did have a bony thumb spike on its hand that was 6 in (14 cm) long. It had powerful arms and could deliver a fearsome blow against an attacker. The spike may also have helped prop up its body against trees when it was reaching for leaves to eat.

◄ HORNS

For *Triceratops*, the best mode of defense was attack, just like the present-day rhinoceros. Its massive head carried an impressive pair of sharp horns that projected from above the eyes and were 3¼-ft (1-m) long. The discovery of a fossil with a healed break suggests that *Triceratops* may well have used the horns for defense rather than for display. Male *Triceratops* may have also used them to fight male rivals. A smaller nose horn and a large, hooked parrotlike beak completed its weaponry.

Bony plates provided some protection to the back

Attackers would have feared the stegosaur's spiked tail

▲ BACK AND TAIL SPIKES

The slow-moving stegosaurs were plant-eaters whose defensive armor and weaponry consisted of long, bony spikes and plates that projected for up to 3¼ ft (1 m) from the tail, back, and shoulders. The long tail carried two pairs of horizontal spikes that could inflict serious damage. The back plates were not strong, but provided some protection to the spine.

TAIL CLUB ▶

One of the most extraordinary defensive weapons of the plant-eating dinosaurs was the tail club of some ankylosaurs. This mass of bone grew on the end of their long tails. Some were 2 ft (60 cm) wide. A large tail club could be swung with enough force to break the leg bone of an attacker.

The bony tail club could break a leg bone

ANKYLOSAURUS

Built like a tank, this dinosaur from Late Cretaceous North America has given its name to a whole group of armored ornithischians—the ankylosaurs. The name means "fused lizard" and refers to the body armor of bony plates embedded in its thick skin—the plates were fused with the skin, not separate from it. These slow-moving plant-eaters were quadrupedal (walking on all fours) and needed the armor as protection against faster and sometimes larger predators.

Tiny plates of bone ringed *Ankylosaurus's* eye sockets and covered its eyelids

The 10-ft- (3-m-) long *Minmi* was one of the smallest ankylosaurs

Osteoderm—a bony plate that fused with the skin

Long tail ended in a heavy club formed from solid bone

❷ ARMORED SKULL

Despite *Ankylosaurus*'s overall bulk, the head was no more than 25 in (64 cm) long. The skull was wide and triangular and protected by spikes on its cheeks and behind its eyes. It had a bulging bony snout with complex air passages inside—no one knows what they were for. With its big beak and small, leaf-shaped teeth at the sides of its jaws, *Ankylosaurus* could only crop vegetation and then swallow it without chewing or grinding.

❶ ANKYLOSAURUS

Although no complete skeleton has been found, *Ankylosaurus* is one the best-known armored dinosaurs—and the largest. Up to 20 ft (6 m) long and weighing 3–4 tons, its squat body was protected by hundreds of bony plates embedded in its skin. It also had bony spikes on its head and a hefty tail club that could be swung at predators with bone-crushing force.

❸ MINMI SKELETON

Early Cretaceous *Minmi* from Australia was one of the smallest ankylosaurs, and specimens include one of the best preserved ankylosaur skeletons. *Minmi* had a unique feature along its back—bony rods called paravertebrae. These may have provided attachment for muscles that strengthened the backbone. Another specimen includes some rarely preserved stomach contents that show that *Minmi* ate fruit.

❹ FOSSILIZED PLATE

Thanks to the discovery of remains with large parts of the body armor preserved, scientists can accurately describe this highly effective form of protection and how it varied from one species of ankylosaur to another. Like *Ankylosaurus*, some had rows of bony plates, known as osteoderms. Others also bristled with bony spikes. Only the belly was unprotected—if predators could get to it.

LIVING TOGETHER

Animals have many good reasons for living and working together in social groups, and dinosaurs were no different. Plant-eaters formed herds whose many eyes and ears provided safety in numbers from predators. Some predators may also have cooperated to tackle large and dangerous prey. Large numbers of fossilized skeletons and bones have been found crowded together at single sites, showing that some dinosaurs lived together and cooperated with each other.

▼ COELOPHYSIS

Hundreds of *Coelophysis* skeletons were found mixed together at Ghost Ranch in New Mexico. It is thought that a whole herd was swept away and drowned by a flash flood. The flock had probably come together during the breeding season, as do many social animals. Some scientists wonder whether these small predators hunted together, but there is no real evidence for this.

Slimly built *Coelophysis* could not have tackled larger prey alone

The footprints of the slow-moving sauropods are parallel, showing that they moved together

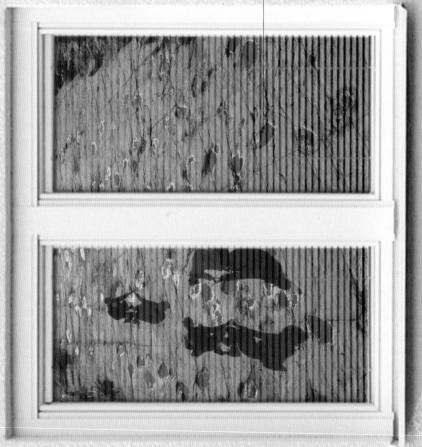

▲ SAUROPOD TRACKS

Scientists often find parallel trackways of many giant sauropods, such as *Diplodocus*, all moving in the same direction at the same time. These provide convincing evidence that these animals were social. They may have come together as they migrated to new feeding or breeding grounds, or for protection from predators. Occasional theropod tracks, recognized by their three-toed shape, are found nearby, suggesting that predators followed the herds.

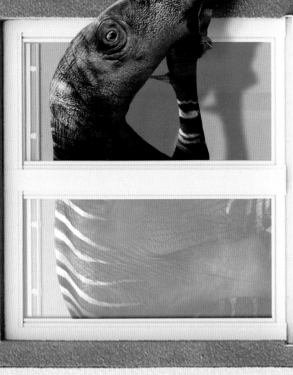

▲ IGUANODON

More than 38 virtually entire adult *Iguanodon* skeletons and a few *Mantellisaurus* skeletons were found in a Belgian coal mine in the late 19th century. The bones show that these ornithopod plant-eaters lived together and fed on the abundant plant growth around the lake. The two species may have herded together, each specializing in a different range of plants.

Even 20-ft- (6-m-) long ceratopsians found safety in numbers

▲ EINIOSAURUS

Hundreds of bones, mostly belonging to 15 individuals of the ceratopsian *Einiosaurus*, have been found in Late Cretaceous rocks of Montana. The fossil remains provide evidence that these 20-ft- (6-m-) long plant-eaters lived in herds, perhaps because this protected them from predators. However, it can be difficult to tell from these bone clusters exactly what happened, and it may be that their remains were washed together by a flood.

Breeding in colonies increased the survival chances of dinosaur babies

▼ MAIASAURA

Fossil remains of numerous bowl-shaped nest mounds and egg fragments have been discovered in Late Cretaceous rocks in Montana. Fossil hatchlings found with the eggs have been identified as those of the duck-billed *Maiasaura*. The females of these plant eating hadrosaurs came together to nest at the same spot generation after generation. Together, their many eyes and ears warned of the approach of predators.

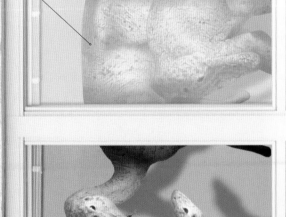

HUNTING AS A PACK

By working together as a pack, predators can tackle animals much larger than themselves and capture prey more easily. But pack-hunting is risky and requires intelligence, communication, and social bonding within the pack. Wolves and lions develop these skills from the moment they are born, by living and playing together and learning from older members of the pack. Perhaps some predatory dinosaurs did the same.

▼ SMALL MEAT-EATERS

In 1947, thousands of fossil bones of *Coelophysis*, a small theropod, were found at Ghost Ranch in New Mexico. Scientists wondered if this was a large pack, but they found no signs of a hunt. Perhaps these *Coelophysis* had gathered for breeding and died in a flash flood.

▲ A DEADLY ATTACK

In the 1990s, the remains of four *Deinonychus* were found alongside a large iguanodontian called *Tenontosaurus* in Montana, US. Scientists wondered whether a pack of *Deinonychus* had attacked the plant-eater, which then killed four of these small theropods before it died of its injuries.

PRESENT-DAY PACKS ▼

Arctic wolves live in family groups of up to 10 animals, sometimes more. Growing up in the pack teaches them to work together to find, attack, and kill large and dangerous prey, such as a 900-lb (400-kg) musk ox. But the chase can be long and exhausting, the prey may turn on its attackers and inflict serious injuries, and not every hunt ends in success.

▲ LARGE MEAT-EATERS

Albertosaurus is usually shown as a solitary predator or scavenger. However, the fossil remains of some 26 individuals of different ages, all found at the same site, may be evidence that they lived in family groups. Perhaps a future find will show that they hunted together, too.

MASS EXTINCTION
The Cretaceous Period ended in catastrophe 66 mya, when an asteroid crashed into Earth. This, and massive volcanic eruptions, led to global climate change that wiped out 85 percent of life, including the dinosaurs.

The end

DEATH OF THE DINOSAURS

The dinosaurs and other groups of Mesozoic reptile, such as the pterosaurs, died out at the end of the Cretaceous Period, 66 million years ago. This was one of several mass extinctions in the long history of life, when many species became extinct at the same time. It was probably caused by the catastrophic collision between an asteroid and Earth. The impact would have thrown up dust clouds that hid the Sun for years, leading to disastrous climate change. Massive volcanic eruptions in India may have made the disaster even worse.

▼ ASTEROID IMPACT

The 6-mile- (10-km-) wide asteroid struck near Chicxulub in Mexico's Yucatán Peninsula. It smashed a hole in the ground 7½ miles (12 km) deep, blasting 12,000 cubic miles (50,000 cubic km) of rock and seawater up into the atmosphere. The debris blocked out sunlight, causing global climate change. As temperatures plunged, plants and animals began to die out.

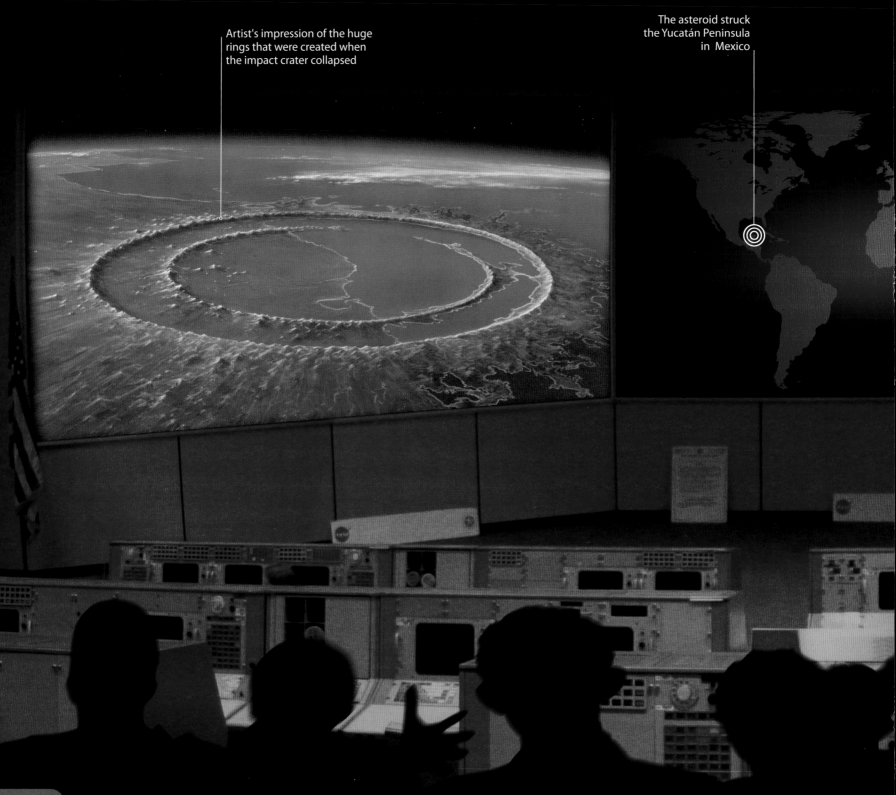

Artist's impression of the huge rings that were created when the impact crater collapsed

The asteroid struck the Yucatán Peninsula in Mexico

▼ THE CRATER TODAY

When the original impact crater collapsed, shockwaves formed three rings measuring 40 miles (70 km), 110 miles (180 km), and 170 miles (300 km) across. The rings were flooded with seawater. At the end of the 1970s scientists looking for oil discovered the rings and worked out what made them.

▼ BOUNDARY LAYER

A thin layer of dark seabed clay marks the end of the Cretaceous Period, but until the 1970s, no one understood its significance. American scientist Walter Alvarez then noticed the high iridium content of the clay. Iridium is rare on Earth, and Alvarez realized that Earth must have been showered with a dusting of iridium from an asteroid impact.

▼ MASSIVE VOLCANO

The end of the Cretaceous Period coincided with the eruption of vast quantities of basalt lavas over the Deccan region of western India. Large-scale volcanic eruptions such as this pump huge quantities of greenhouse gases into the atmosphere, causing global climate change. This may well have contributed to the dinosaurs' extinction.

Computer-generated gravity map of the buried crater site at Chicxulub

A dark layer of iridium-enriched clay marks the boundary between the Cretaceous and Paleogene periods

Coin placed on the layer shows how thin it is

The Deccan's Western Ghats formed from eruptions 66 mya

The site of the major volcanic eruptions in western India

SURVIVORS

The dinosaurs are the most famous victims of the end-Cretaceous extinction, and their descendants—the birds—are the most famous survivors. Other major Mesozoic reptile groups, however, such as the pterosaurs and plesiosaurs, were also wiped out. Yet there survived a significant number of reptile groups that still populate the Earth today. They include the crocodiles, turtles, lizards, and snakes. Other important survivors include the mammals, bony fish, flowering plants, and the insects that pollinate them.

❶ NAUTILUS

The pearly *Nautilus* is a shelled cephalopod—a type of mollusk that has a large head and a set of arms or tentacles—and closely related to octupuses and squid. This predator lives in the Indian Ocean and is the sole survivor of an ancient group of nautiloids that evolved in Cambrian times almost 500 mya. The ammonites, another group of cephalopods closely related to the nautiloids, became extinct at the end of the Cretaceous Period.

❷ GASTORNIS

As tall as a man, this flightless bird lived in the tropical forests of North America and Europe 50 mya. It belonged to a group of birds that evolved in the Late Cretaceous Period and still survives in the form of present-day waterfowl such as ducks, geese, and swans.

❸ ATURIA

This nautiloid lived in the Paleogene Period, which followed the age of the dinosaurs, and survived into the Early Neogene Period, about 20 mya. Found worldwide, it probably swam in open seas and fed on small fish and crustaceans.

❹ PUPPIGERUS

Sea turtles evolved in the Early Cretaceous Period from a group of Late Triassic reptiles and survived the end-Cretaceous extinction. *Puppigerus,* which lived in subtropical seas 55–40 mya, was 35 in (90 cm) long and had huge eyes.

BIRDS CONTINUED

After evolving from small, theropod dinosaurs in the Jurassic Period, Cretaceous birds continued to diversify into distinct groups. Gradually, they lost the primitive features such as the long, bony tail and toothed jaws seen in *Archaeopteryx* on pages 58–59. Many birds disappeared in the end-Cretaceous extinction, but some species survived. Over the past 66 million years, their descendants have flourished and there are more than 9,000 species alive today.

❶ HESPERORNIS

The Late Cretaceous *Hesperornis* was a large, 3¼-ft- (1-m-) long seabird with tiny wings. Although it could not fly, it was an expert swimmer. It used its huge, long-toed feet to paddle out to sea, dive deep, and chase fish and squid, which it grabbed in its long, toothy beak. Whenever *Hesperornis* came ashore to nest, it probably could not walk and had to push itself along on its belly. It became extinct at the end of the Cretaceous Period.

Long, slender neck and body

❶

Toothed beak

Long legs and toes

Very small wings

Vegavis probably had a ducklike, toothless bill

Large head and toothed jaws

❷

❸

❷ ICHTHYORNIS

Another Late Cretaceous seabird, *Ichthyornis* was 2 ft (60 cm) long, the size of a large seagull, although its head and beak were much larger. The middle of the beak was lined with small, curved teeth, like those of the marine reptiles called mosasaurs, and it used these to catch hold of fish and other slippery prey. It had webbed feet with short claws, and—unlike *Archaeopteryx*—large chest muscles attached to a tall ridge on its breastbone. This bird was a powerful swimmer and flyer.

❸ VEGAVIS

This bird was one of the oldest members of the major group known as waterfowl, which includes present-day ducks and geese. When its fossil remains were found in 1992, they confirmed that some of today's bird families had already evolved before the end-Cretaceous extinction. *Vegavis* was 2 ft (60 cm) long, about the size of a mallard duck, and lived in Antarctica in the Late Cretaceous Period, when climates were much warmer than they are today.

❻ DINORNIS

The giant moa from New Zealand stood 12 ft (3.6 m) tall, making it the tallest bird ever known, and weighed about 620 lb (280 kg). Males were smaller than females. These flightless plant-eaters were hunted to extinction by humans in the 16th century CE. They belong to the paleognath group of birds that first evolved during the Paleogene Period that followed the Cretaceous. This group still survives in the form of flightless birds such as ostriches, emus, and kiwis.

Long neck allowed the giant moa to reach a range of vegetation, high and low

❼ TITANIS

Broken, incomplete fossils of *Titanis* suggest that it was a huge, 6½-ft- (2-m-) tall, flightless carnivore with long powerful legs and a huge hooked beak. It lived 5–2 mya and was one of the last survivors of the flightless group known as "terror birds." The group evolved in South America soon after the end of the Cretaceous Period and later spread to North America.

Single claw on each wing

Huge horned beak

❹ IBEROMESORNIS

Sparrow-sized *Iberomesornis* had advanced features, such as a short tail, powerful chest muscles suited to flying, and a backward-pointing toe on each foot that allowed for perching. But it also had more primitive features, such as a single claw on each wing. It belongs to a group of primitive birds that evolved in Early Cretaceous times and became extinct at the end of that period.

❺ PRESBYORNIS

This long-necked, long-legged, Early Paleogene bird was closely related to waterfowl, such as ducks and geese. Numerous fossils, including nests and eggs, have been found in sites that were once shallow lakes. Perhaps *Presbyornis* was a wading bird, living in large lakeside colonies, and used its ducklike beak to filter small organisms from the water's edge.

EARLY MAMMALS

From mice to whales and humans, all mammals are descended from an ancient group of reptiles known as the synapsids. The first mammals appeared in the Late Triassic Period. They were tiny animals that came out at night to feed and were warm-blooded, active, and well insulated with hair. These features helped them to survive in the shadow of the dinosaurs, which were mostly active by day. After the dinosaurs were wiped out, larger mammals evolved in the Paleogene Period that followed the Cretaceous. All the largest animals alive today are mammals.

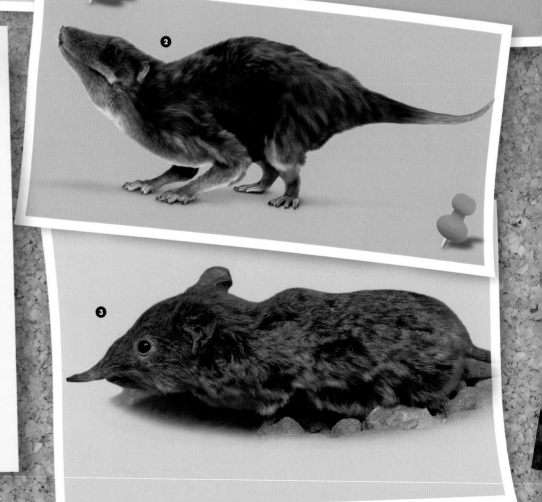

❶ MORGANUCODON
This was one of the earliest of the primitive mammals. It was 3½ in (9 cm) long, looked like a large shrew, and hunted insects at night. It probably laid eggs, just as the platypus and other monotremes (egg-laying mammals) do today.

❷ EOMAIA
A single, perfect fossil from China shows that Early Cretaceous *Eomaia* was 4 in (10 cm) long, furry, a good climber, and an insect-eater. Its name means "dawn mother" and its bones show that it was more closely related to placental mammals, which give birth to live young, than to the egg-laying mammals.

❸ ZALAMBDALESTES
This rat-sized insect-eater from Late Cretaceous Mongolia was 9½ in (24 cm) long. It had long legs suited to running and jumping, a long narrow snout, and teeth that grew continuously throughout its life—like those of rodents. It was one of the earliest placental mammals.

❹ PHENACODUS

In the Paleogene Period, 66–23 mya, early hoofed mammals known as the condylarths grazed in grasslands and woodlands. One species, *Phenacodus*, was 4½ ft (1.4 m) long. It carried most of its weight on three long middle toes, each of which ended in a small, blunt hoof.

❺ ICARONYCTERIS

The Paleogene *Icaronycteris* was one of the earliest bats. It was 5½ in (14 cm) long and had a 15-in (37-cm) wingspan. Like present-day bats, it used echolocation to catch insects at night—one fossil has moth scales in its stomach.

❻ DARWINIUS

Primates, the group of mammals that now includes monkeys and humans, first appeared just as the dinosaurs became extinct. They only began to flourish in the Paleogene Period. Among them were agile climbers, such as the lemurlike *Darwinius*.

LIVING FOSSILS

Earth's fossil record shows us that today's rich diversity of life is just the tip of a vast family tree. Over hundreds of millions of years, most of the plants and animals that evolved have become extinct, but some have survived with very little change. These "living fossils" are so well adapted to their environment that there is little or no need to change. Sometimes a gap in the fossil record gives a false impression of a species' extinction—until survivors are found tucked away in protective environments known as refugia.

❶ GINKGO

The distinctive fan-shaped leaves of fossil ginkgos have been found in rocks dating back to the Early Jurassic Period. The tree-sized ginkgos are seed plants, which evolved before the flowering plants and became widespread during the Jurassic and Cretaceous periods. Then they seemed to have died out in Pliocene times about 3 mya. However, one species has survived, growing wild in the mountains of China, and is now planted in parks and gardens worldwide.

❷ BRACHIOPODS

This ancient group of seabed-dwelling shellfish first evolved about 525 mya, in the Early Cambrian Period and produced about 12,000 fossil species before being reduced to the 330 species alive today. One of the earliest groups of brachiopods included the lingulates, whose shell shape and lifestyle has not changed in 500 million years. The body is encased by two valves (shells) and attached to the seabed by a fleshy stalk.

Today's African giant black millipede grows to around 14 in (35 cm) long

❸ MILLIPEDES

Although their name means "1,000 feet," these creepy-crawlies only have 100–300 legs and move slowly through the soil, where they feed on rotting plant debris. They were among the first animals to colonize the land—their fossil record goes back at least 428 million years to the Silurian Period. By the Early Carboniferous Period 350 mya, they had evolved into giant forms such as the 8½-ft- (2-m-) long *Arthropleura*.

Fossil *Lingula* shell

❹ COELACANTHS

The most famous living fossils of all are the coelacanths. They belong to an ancient group of lobe-finned fish, which originated in the Early Devonian Period about 400 mya. Their long fossil record seemed to show that coelacanths died out in the end-Cretaceous extinction, along with the dinosaurs. But in 1938, fishermen in South Africa caught a living specimen in a shark net in the Indian Ocean, and in 1997, a second species was found in Indonesia.

❺ VELVET WORMS

The 180 living species of velvet worm belong to a group of animal called the onychophorans, which originated in the early Cambrian Period about 500 mya. Today, these caterpillarlike and sized creatures, with soft segmented bodies and numerous stubby feet, are forest-floor predators living in the leaf litter of tropical forests in the southern hemisphere. However, their Cambrian ancestors were entirely marine and their fossil record is very sparse.

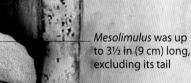

Mesolimulus was up to 3½ in (9 cm) long, excluding its tail

❻ HORSESHOE CRABS

Despite their name, these ancient animals are more closely related to spiders and scorpions than crabs. They first evolved in the Late Ordovician Period around 450 mya and have hardly changed since then. The body and five pairs of legs are protected by a horseshoe-shaped shell called a carapace, which is molted as the animal grows, and the stiff tail ends in a sharp tip like a spear. *Mesolimulus* lived on the Late Jurassic seabed, where it hunted worms and shellfish.

Late Cretaceous *Macropoma* was once thought to be the last-known coelacanth

Glossary

ADAPTATION
A modification of an animal or plant that evolved in response to its environment or way of life.

AMBER
The fossil form of sticky tree resin that may contain well preserved insects and other organisms.

ANCESTOR
An animal or plant species from which a more recent species has evolved.

ANKYLOSAURS
Four-legged, plant-eating ornithischian dinosaurs with body armor of bony plates and spikes, from the Mid Jurassic to the Late Cretaceous Periods.

ARCHOSAURS
A large group of reptiles that first evolved in the Early Triassic Period and includes dinosaurs, pterosaurs, and crocodilians.

ASTEROID
A rocky or metallic object that orbits the Sun, left over from the formation of the planets. An asteroid crashing into Earth probably contributed to the end-Cretaceous mass extinction.

AVIAN DINOSAURS
Feathered dinosaurs, with wings that were primarily used in flapping flight. Avian dinosaurs now include about 10,000 living species, also known as birds. Non-avian dinosaurs died out at the end of the Cretaceous Period.

BIPEDAL
Walking on two legs.

CARNIVORE
An animal that eats only meat.

CERATOPSIANS
Four-legged, plant-eating ornithischian dinosaurs with horns and beaks. This group lived from the Late Jurassic to the Late Cretaceous Periods.

CLIMATE CHANGE
Major change to global weather conditions that may last for millions of years. Climate change is thought to have led to the end-Cretaceous mass extinction.

COLD-BLOODED
Describes an animal whose body temperature rises and falls with changes in the temperature of its surroundings. Warm-blooded animals maintain a constant body temperature.

COPROLITE
Fossilized animal dung.

CRETACEOUS PERIOD
The third and final period of the Mesozoic Era, lasting from 145 to 66 million years ago.

CROCODILIANS
A group of reptiles that includes today's crocodiles and alligators. They and their many extinct relatives are together known as crocodylomorphs, which first appeared at the same time as the dinosaurs and belong to the archosaur group of reptiles.

DESCENDANT
An animal or plant species that evolved from an earlier species (its ancestor).

DINOSAURS
A large group of archosaur reptiles with upright limbs that dominated life on land for 160 million years, from the Late Triassic Period to the end of the Cretaceous Period. Birds are their direct descendants.

DIPLODOCIDS
Giant, long-necked, whip-tailed sauropod dinosaurs from the Late Jurassic Period, including some of the largest dinosaurs, such as *Diplodocus*. Their hind legs were longer than their front legs.

DROMAEOSAURS
Birdlike, two-legged, fast-running, and predatory theropod dinosaurs of small to medium size, with an extra-large claw on the second toe. This group lived between the Mid Jurassic and Late Cretaceous Periods and gave rise to the first birds.

EMBRYO
An animal or plant in the early stage of development from an egg or seed. Some fossil eggs still contain an embryo.

EVOLUTION
The gradual change of an animal or plant species over a long time, which may result in new species.

EXCAVATION
Digging out and removing fossils or other objects from the ground.

EXTINCTION
The dying out of a plant or animal species. Extinction can happen naturally, as a result of competition between species, replacement by newly evolved species, changes in the environment, or natural disasters (such as an asteroid impact), or as a result of hunting and destruction of habitat by humans.

FLOWERING PLANTS
Seed-producing plants that reproduce by means of flowers and fruit containing seeds. They first evolved in the Early Cretaceous Period.

FOSSIL
The remains or traces of a dead organism preserved in rock.

FOSSILIZATION
The process by which plant and animal remains become buried and preserved in rock.

GASTROLITH
A stone swallowed by an animal, such as a plant-eating dinosaur, that aids the digestion of food by grinding it to a pulp.

GIGANTOTHERMY
A condition of large, cold-blooded animals whose bulk maintains a more constant body heat than smaller cold-blooded animals.

GIZZARD
A part of the digestive system in some animals. Its muscular walls help grind up plant food, often aided by gastroliths.

HADROSAURS
Duck-billed, plant-eating ornithischian dinosaurs of the Late Cretaceous Period. Some had distinctive, bony crests.

HATCHLING
A newborn animal that has emerged from a shelled egg.

HERBIVORE
An animal that eats only plants.

ICHTHYOSAURS
Dolphin-shaped, predatory sea-dwelling reptiles that were common in the Mesozoic Era.

IGUANODONTIDS
Large, plant-eating, ornithopod dinosaurs with long, horselike faces, named after *Iguanodon*. They lived from the Mid Jurassic to Late Cretaceous Periods and included the hadrosaurs.

INVERTEBRATE
An animal without a backbone.

JURASSIC PERIOD
The second period of the Mesozoic Era, lasting from 201 to 145 million years ago.

MAMMALS
Warm-blooded vertebrate animals that feed their young on milk and have skin covered in hair. They originated in the Late Triassic Period.

MARINE
Describes animals and plants living in the sea.

MASS EXTINCTION
The extinction of huge numbers of species at the same time.

MESOZOIC ERA
The era lasting from 252 to 66 million years ago, comprising the Triassic, Jurassic, and Cretaceous periods.

MOSASAURS
Large, sea-dwelling predatory reptiles with long snouts, paddle-shaped limbs, and a flat tail. They lived during the Late Cretaceous Period.

MYA
Million years ago.

NOCTURNAL
Describes animals that are active during the night.

NOTHOSAURS
Large, sea-dwelling, predatory reptiles in the Triassic Period. They had a lizardlike body and four legs with webbed feet and may have come ashore like seals.

OMNIVORE
An animal that eats both plant matter and meat.

ORNITHISCHIAN
"Bird-hipped." One of two major divisions in the dinosaur family tree (see also Saurischian). In ornithischian dinosaurs, the pelvis (hip bone) had a pubis bone pointing downward and backward, as in the birds. The ornithischians were plant-eaters.

ORNITHOPODS
Plant-eating, mainly two-legged ornithischian dinosaurs with long hind limbs. This group included the hypsilophodonts, iguanodontids, and duck-billed hadrosaurs and lived from the Mid Jurassic to the Late Cretaceous Periods.

OVIRAPTOROSAURS
Small, feathered, theropod dinosaurs of the Cretaceous Period, with parrotlike beaks. Mistakenly named "egg thieves."

PACHYCEPHALOSAURS
Two-legged, ornithischian dinosaurs with thick, domed skulls. This group included plant-eaters and omnivores, and lived mostly in the Late Cretaceous Period.

PALEONTOLOGY
The study of fossilized plants and animals. Scientists who specialize in this study are paleontologists.

PANGAEA
The supercontinent that existed in the Late Paleozoic and Early Mesozoic Eras.

PELVIS
The part of an animal's skeleton that forms the hips and connects the hind limbs to the backbone.

PLACENTAL MAMMALS
Mammals that are nourished by a placenta within their mother's body before birth.

PLESIOSAURS
Large, predatory marine reptiles with flipperlike limbs that lived between the Early Jurassic and Late Cretaceous periods. Many had long necks and tiny heads. Others (pliosaurs) had short necks and large heads.

PLIOSAURS
These short-necked, predatory marine reptiles had large heads and crocodilelike teeth. They were plesiosaurs and lived between the Early Jurassic and Late Cretaceous periods.

PREDATOR
An animal that hunts other live animals for food.

PREY
An animal that is hunted for food.

PRIMITIVE
At an early stage of evolution.

PTEROSAURS
Huge flying reptiles that, like the dinosaurs, were archosaurs, originated in the Late Triassic Period, and became extinct at the end of the Cretaceous Period.

QUADRUPED
An animal that walks on all fours.

REPTILES
Mostly cold-blooded animals with scaly skin that reproduce by laying eggs. Reptiles originated in the Late Carboniferous Period, gave rise to the dinosaurs, and include today's lizards, snakes, turtles, and crocodiles.

SAURISCHIAN
"Lizard-hipped." One of the two major divisions in the dinosaur family tree (see also Ornithischian). In saurischian dinosaurs, the pelvis (hip bones) has the pubis bone pointing forward, as in the lizards. All meat-eating dinosaurs were saurischians.

SAUROPODS
Large, four-legged, plant-eating saurischian dinosaurs with long necks and tails and small heads.

They and their more primitive relatives, the prosauropods, are known as sauropodomorphs. They lived from the Late Triassic to the Late Cretaceous periods and included the largest land animals of all time.

SCAVENGER
An animal that feeds on the meat of another animal that has been killed by predators or died naturally.

SEDIMENT
Material such as sand and mud deposited by wind, water, or ice, which may then harden into rock. Most fossils are found in sedimentary rock.

SEED PLANTS
Plants that reproduce by means of seeds, including conifers, cycads, and flowering plants. They originated in the Late Devonian Period.

SPECIES
A type of animal or plant. Individuals of a species can breed together and produce fertile offspring. There were more than 1,000 species of dinosaur.

SPINOSAURIDS
Large theropods with a long crocodilelike skull and bony "sail" structure on the back. Spinosaurids emerged in the Late Jurassic Period and died out in the Late Cretaceous.

STEGOSAURS
Four-legged, plant-eating ornithischian dinosaurs with two rows of plates or spines on their backs. This group originated in the Mid Jurassic Period and died out in the Early Cretaceous.

STRATA
Layers of sedimentary rocks laid down over time in which fossils may be preserved.

SUPERCONTINENT
A cluster of continents brought together by Earth's shifting plates into one giant landmass.

TETRAPOD
A backboned animal with four limbs, arranged in two pairs—arms, legs, or wings. Amphibians, reptiles, mammals, and birds are

all tetrapods that evolved from a fishlike ancestor in the Mid Devonian Period.

THEROPODS
Two-legged, saurischian dinosaurs that were predatory carnivores and ranged in size from the tiny *Microraptor* to the colossal *Tyrannosaurus rex*. They originated in the Late Triassic Period and gave rise to the birds.

TITANOSAURS
Giant, plant-eating sauropods with long necks and small heads, which originated in the Late Jurassic Period and died out in the Late Cretaceous.

TRACE FOSSIL
A mark or impression made by a creature, rather than the remains of the creature itself, and then preserved in rock. Trace fossils include footprints, bite marks, and droppings.

TRIASSIC PERIOD
The first of three periods in the Mesozoic Era, lasting from 252 to 201 million years ago.

TYRANNOSAURS
Large, two-legged, predatory theropod saurischians with a massive skull, long legs and tail, and tiny arms. Among the last and best-known dinosaurs of all, they lived in the Late Cretaceous.

VERTEBRAE
The linked bones forming the backbone of a vertebrate animal.

VERTEBRATE
An animal with a backbone, or spine, made up of vertebrae. Vertebrates arose in Cambrian times and include all fish, amphibians, reptiles, birds, and mammals.

WARM-BLOODED
Describes an animal that maintains a constant internal body temperature. Unlike a cold-blooded animal, its body temperature does not change with the temperature of its surroundings.

WINGSPAN
The distance from the tip of one wing to the tip of the other when both wings are outstretched.

Index

Acknowledgments

DK would like to thank:
Joe Fullman and Rob Colson for editorial assistance; David John for proofreading; Helen Peters for preparing the index; and Vikas Chauhan and Jyotsna Khosla for design assistance.

The publisher would like to thank the following for their kind permission to reproduce their photographs:

Key:
a-above; b-below/bottom; c-centre; f-far; l-left; r-right; t-top

1–5: The American Museum of Natural History; Bedrock Studios; Centaur Studios – modelmakers; Graham High at Centaur Studios – modelmaker; The Hunterian Museum (University of Glasgow); Institute of Geology and Palaeontology, Tubingen, Germany; James Stevenson / Donks Models –modelmaker; Jeremy Hunt at Centaur Studios – modelmaker; Jon Hughes, John Holmes – modelmaker ; Jonathan Hately – modelmaker; The Leicester Museum; Natural History Museum, London; Peter Minister, Digital Sculptor; Royal Tyrrell Museum of Palaeontology, Alberta, Canada; Russell Gooday; Sedgwick Museum of Geology, Cambridge; Staatliches Museum fur Naturkunde Stuttgart; Tim Ridley / Robert L. Braun – modelmaker; 4 Dorling Kindersley: Peter Minister, Digital Sculpto (tr). **5 Corbis:** Mike Agliolo (tr/meteor). **Dorling Kindersley:** Peter Minister, Digital Sculptor (tl). **Getty Images:** Willard Clay / Photographer's Choice (tl/background). **Science Photo Library:** Mark Garlick (tr). **8 Dorling Kindersley:** Crystal Palace Park, London (c). **Dreamstime.com:** Li Fang (br); Dmitriy Shironosov (bc). **8–9 Dreamstime.com:** Alexandre Miguel Da Silva Nunes (background). **9 Dorling Kindersley:** Natural History Museum, London (cl). **Dreamstime.com:** Dmitriy Shironosov (bc). **10 Dorling Kindersley:** David Donkin – modelmaker (cl, c, clb). **Dreamstime.com:** Duron0123 (cr/DVD); Rafael Angel Irusta Machin (bl, tr, br); Kurvina (cr, br/Wire). **Getty Images:** Marcello Paternostro / AFP (tr/volcano). **10–11 Dreamstime.com:** Donsimon (t); Zts (c, bc/Silver DVD); Duron0123 (bc); Shevchenkon (Background). **11 Dreamstime.com:** Duron0123 (c); Rafael Angel Irusta Machin (tc, bc); Kurvina (c/wire); Andrew Kazmierski (tr). **Getty Images:** Barcroft Media (tc/Ice). **Science Photo Library:** Mark Garlick (bc/Extinction). **12 Dorling Kindersley:** John Downes / John Holmes – modelmaker / Natural History Museum, London (c); Jon Hughes (tr). **13 Dorling Kindersley:** Jon Hughes (bl); Peter Minister, Digital Sculptor (cl). **14 Dreamstime.com:** Antonel (cl). **University Museum of Zoology, Cambridge:** Richard Hammond – modelmaker (c). **14–15 Dreamstime.com:** Nilsz; Readi24 (background). **15 Dorling Kindersley:** Jon Hughes & Russell Gooday (c). **16 Dorling Kindersley:** Jon Hughes (tl, cl); Tim Ridley / Robert L. Braun – modelmaker (tl/Herrerasaurus). **Dreamstime.com:** Rushour (tl/board). **16–17 Dreamstime.com:** Alex Evans (bc). **Science Photo Library:** Walter Myers (c). **17 Dorling Kindersley:** Jon Hughes (tl); Jon Hughes & Russell Gooday (r). **18 Dorling Kindersley:** Jon Hughes (bl); Peter Minister, Digital Sculptor (tl, c). **Dreamstime.com:** Rushour (tl/board). **18–19 Science Photo Library:** Richard Bizley (Background). **19 Dorling Kindersley:** Jon Hughes (br); Peter Minister, Digital Sculptor (cr). **20 Dorling Kindersley:** Jon Hughes (l, bc); Jonathan Hateley – modelmaker (tl/dinosaur). **Dreamstime.com:** Rushour (tl). **21 Dorling Kindersley:** Jon Hughes (bc). **22 Dorling Kindersley:** Jon Hughes & Russell Gooday (b). **22–23 Dreamstime.com:** Ian Francis (background); Jakub Krechowicz; Natalia Siverina (c). **23 Dorling Kindersley:** Peter Minister, Digital Sculptor (bc); Tim Ridley / Robert L. Braun – modelmaker (tc). **Dreamstime.com:** Waxart (tr). **24 Dorling Kindersley:** Peter Minister, Digital Sculptor. **24–25 Dreamstime.com:** Ahmet Ihsan Ariturk (background); Videowokart (b). **25 Corbis:** Louie Psihoyos (cr). **Dorling Kindersley:** Peter Minister, Digital Sculptor (tr, cra). **26 Dorling Kindersley:** Jon Hughes & Russell Gooday (crb); Peter Minister, Digital Sculptor (br, bc). **26–27 Getty Images:** National Geographic / Jeffrey L. Osborn (bc). **27 Dorling Kindersley:** Jon Hughes & Russell Gooday (l, bl); Jon Hughes (bc). **Dreamstime.com:** Szerdahelyi Adam (r). **Science Photo Library:** Christian Darkin (c). **28 Dorling Kindersley:** Robert L. Braun – modelmaker (tl). **28–29 Dreamstime.com:** Lucidwaters (Background). **29 Dorling Kindersley:** Peter Minister, Digital Sculptor (c). **30–31 Dorling Kindersley:** Peter Minister, Digital Sculptor (c). **Dreamstime.com:** Amabrao (background). **31 Dorling Kindersley:** Sedgwick Museum of Geology, Cambridge (bc). **Dreamstime.com:** Johannesk (br). **32–33 Dorling Kindersley:** Jon Hughes (c). **Dreamstime.com:** Brad Calkins; (paper). **34 Corbis:** Francesc Muntada (br). **Dorling Kindersley:** Natural History Museum, London (c, c/teeth). **34–35 Dreamstime.com:** Sommersby (Background). **35 Derek Siveter:** (cl). **36 Dorling Kindersley:** Natural History Museum, London (c). **Getty Images:** Spencer Platt (br). **36–37 Dorling Kindersley:** Natural History Museum, London (background). **37 Dorling Kindersley:** Natural History Museum, London (tl, cr). **naturepl.com:** Jean E. Roche (bl). **38 Dorling Kindersley:** Natural History Museum, London (bc). **38–39 Corbis:** Louie Psihoyos (c). **Dreamstime.com:** Summersea (c/Frame). **39 Corbis:** William James Warren / Science Faction (tr); Louie Psihoyos / Science Faction (bl, c). **40 Corbis:** Louie Psihoyos (bl). **41 Dorling Kindersley:** Jon Hughes (tr); Natural History Museum, London (b). **42–43 Dorling Kindersley:** Peter Minister, Digital Sculpto. **44 Dorling Kindersley:** The American Museum of Natural History (tr). **Dreamstime.com:** Netfalls (bl). **45 Dorling Kindersley:** Natural History Museum, London (tr); Royal Tyrrell Museum of Palaeontology, Alberta, Canada (c). **46–47 Science Photo Library:** Peter Menzel (bc). **48 Dorling Kindersley:** Hunterian Museum (University of Glasgow) (b). **Dreamstime.com:** Olivier Le Queinec (tl). **49 Alamy Images:** Phil Degginger (br). **Dorling Kindersley:** The American Museum of Natural History (c). **Dreamstime.com:** Dimitri Zimmer (r). **Getty Images:** O. Louis Mazzatenta / National Geographic (tl). **50 Dreamstime.com:** Olena Chyrko (tl). **51 Dorling Kindersley:** Jon Hughes (bl). **52 Dreamstime.com:** Trosamange (b). **52–53 Dorling Kindersley:** Peter Minister, Digital Sculptor. **Dreamstime.com:** Rvc5pogod (b). **Getty Images:** Spencer Platt (tc); Siri Stafford / The Image Bank (background). **53 Dreamstime.com:** Carlos Arranz (crb); Joseph Gough (bl). **54 Dorling Kindersley:** Natural History Museum, London (cr). **54–55 Dreamstime.com:** Py2000 (background). **55 Dorling Kindersley:** Royal Tyrrell Museum of Palaeontology, Alberta, Canada (crb). **56–57 Corbis:** Viaframe (background). **57 Dorling Kindersley:** Jon Hughes (clb). **58 Dorling Kindersley:** Jon Hughes (bc); Peter Minister, Digital Sculptor (bl). **Dreamstime.com:** Chaoss (tr, bl/paper, br); Joseph Gough (tl). **58–59 Dorling Kindersley:** Peter Minister, Digital Sculptor (c). **Dreamstime.com:** Pedro Antonio Salaverría Calahorra (background). **59 Corbis:** Louie Psihoyos (tl/Feather Fossil). **Dorling Kindersley:** Natural History Museum, London (br). **Dreamstime.com:** Chaoss (tl, bl, cr). **60 Dorling Kindersley:** Graham High at Centaur Studios – modelmaker (cl); Robert L. Braun – modelmaker (br). **Dreamstime.com:** Anna Jurkovska (bl, tc). **61 Corbis:** Louie Psihoyos (bc). **Dorling Kindersley:** John Holmes – modelmaker (cr). **62 Dorling Kindersley:** Institute und Museum fur Geologie und Palaontologie der Universitat Tubingen, Germany (tr). **Dreamstime.com:** Irochka (br). **Getty Images:** Foodcollection (cr). **62–63 Dreamstime.com:** Kritiya (Background). **63 Dorling Kindersley:** Peter Minister, Digital Sculptor (c, cl). **Dreamstime.com:** Irochka. **64 Dreamstime.com:** Joseph Gough (tc); Twickey (bl). **Getty Images:** Encyclopaedia Britannica / Universal Images Group (cl). **65 Dorling Kindersley:** Natural History Museum, London (br); Peter Minister, Digital Sculptor (br/egg, tl/Face). **Dreamstime.com:** Joseph Gough (tl, tr); Twickey (cr, bc). **66 Alamy Images:** Alberto Paredes (clb). **Dorling Kindersley:** Peter Minister, Digital Sculptor (cr). **Getty Images:** Tony Waltham / Robert Harding (cr). **Dr Howard Falcon-Lang:** (cl). **66–67 Dreamstime.com:** Alek Kringstad (Background); Glenn Nagel (b). **67 Dreamstime.com:** Sanjmur (cr). **68 University Museum of Zoology, Cambridge:** Richard Hammond – modelmaker (cl). **68–69 Dorling Kindersley:** Jon Hughes (c). **69 Dorling Kindersley:** Jon Hughes / Bedrock Studios (cr). **70–71 Dreamstime.com:** Azimnik (tc); Duccio (background). **71 Dorling Kindersley:** Natural History Museum, London (cra). **72 Dorling Kindersley:** Bedrock Studios (c). **72–73 Dreamstime.com:** Puma330. **73 Dorling Kindersley:** Peter Minister, Digital Sculptor (c). **74 Alamy Images:** Pictorial Press (br). **Dreamstime.com:** Ivan Gusev (br/kite); Mfinch1 (clb). **76 Corbis:** Louie Psihoyos (c, tc); Reuters (br). **76–77 Dreamstime.com:** Baronoskie (background). **77 Dorling Kindersley:** Natural History Museum, London (bl). **78 Dorling Kindersley:** Jon Hughes & Russell Gooday (cl, br). **Dreamstime.com:** Pixbox77 (Background). **79 Dorling Kindersley:** Peter Minister, Digital Sculptor (bl). **Dreamstime.com:** Dmitry Pichugin (background). **82–83 Dorling Kindersley:** Peter Minister, Digital Sculptor. **Getty Images:** Willard Clay / Photographer's Choice (background). **84 Dorling Kindersley:** Royal Tyrrell Museum of Palaeontology, Alberta, Canada (cr). **Dreamstime.com:** Robert Byron (bl/clipboard). **Science Photo Library:** Roger Harris (bl). **84–85 Dreamstime.com:** James Steidl (Background). **85 Dreamstime.com:** Vladimir Sazonov (br). **86 Dreamstime.com:** Artushfoto (cl); Yarkoa (tr); Brian Hendricks (bc); Christian Mueringer (br). **86–87 Dreamstime.com:** Sarayusu (Background). **87 Dorling Kindersley:** Peter Minister, Digital Sculptor (c). **Dreamstime.com:** (br); Ferli Achirulli Kamaruddin (r); Christian Mueringer (bl). **88 Dorling Kindersley:** Royal Tyrrell Museum of Palaeontology, Alberta, Canada (bc). **Dreamstime.com:** Cebas1 (bc/board); Splosh (t). **88–89 Dorling Kindersley:** Peter Minister, Digital Sculptor. **Dreamstime.com:** Hans Slegers (bc). **89 Dorling Kindersley:** The American Museum of Natural History (tr). **90 Dorling Kindersley:** Jon Hughes & Russell Gooday (r). **Dreamstime.com:** Pavel Losevsky (bl, tr). **90–91 Dorling Kindersley:** Jon Hughes (c). **91 Dreamstime.com:** Pavel Losevsky (tl, tr, br). **92 Dreamstime.com:** Berci (tr). **92–93 Dreamstime.com:** Dzianis Kazlouski (background); Summersea (b). **93 Dreamstime.com:** Berci (tl, tc). **94 Dorling Kindersley:** Jon Hughes (crb); Peter Minister, Digital Sculptor (cl). **94–95 Corbis:** Ashley Cooper (b). **Dreamstime.com:** Pabkov (t); Daniel Vincek (Background). **95 Corbis:** Louie Psihoyos (cra). **Dorling Kindersley:** Robert L. Braun – modelmaker (c). **Dreamstime.com:** Alexander Raths (t). **Getty Images:** Dan Kitwood (b). **96 Dorling Kindersley:** Natural History Museum, London (bc, tc, tr). **96–97 Dorling Kindersley:** Peter Minister, Digital Sculptor (background). **Dreamstime.com:** Araraadt (background1). **97 Dorling Kindersley:** Staatliches Museum fur Naturkunde Stuttgart (cl). **Dreamstime.com:** Bravajulia (t); Elnur (br). **98 Dreamstime.com:** Radekdrewek (tr). **98–99 Dreamstime.com:** Songquan Deng (background). **99 Dreamstime.com:** Davinci (tr); trekandshoot (tl); Olgaruza (c); Senensc (tc/people). **100 Dorling Kindersley:** Peter Minister, Digital Sculptor (l). **Dreamstime.com:** Cebas1 (bc). **Fotolia:** Zharastudio (br). **100–101 Corbis:** Nick Ledger / JAI (background). **Dorling Kindersley:** Jon Hughes & Russell Gooday (c). **Fotolia:** swisshippo (tc). **101 Dorling Kindersley:** Jon Hughes (tr); Staatliches Museum fur Naturkunde Stuttgart (crb). **Dreamstime.com:** Cebas1 (bl, br); Dimdimich (tc). **102–103 Dorling Kindersley:** Peter Minister, Digital Sculptor (c). **Getty Images:** Willard Clay / Photographer's Choice (background). **103 Dorling Kindersley:** Naturmuseum Senckenburg, Frankfurt (t). **Dreamstime.com:** Feverpitched. **104 Dorling Kindersley:** The American Museum of Natural History (bl); Natural History Museum, London (tr). **Dreamstime.com:** Py2000 (bc). **104–105 Getty Images:** Sandro Di Carlo Darsa / PhotoAlto Agency RF Collections (background). **105 Dorling Kindersley:** Royal Tyrrell Museum of Palaeontology, Alberta, Canada (cr). **106 Dorling Kindersley:** Natural History Museum, London (c); Royal Tyrrell Museum of Palaeontology, Alberta, Canada (cl); Queensland Museum, Brisbane, Australia (tr). **Dreamstime.com:** Emberiza; Kamyshko (c/background). **106–107 Dorling Kindersley:** Jon Hughes & Russell Gooday (b). **107 Dreamstime.com:** Gino Crescoli (cr); Liquidphoto (tl). **108 Corbis:** Louie Psihoyos (br). **Dorling Kindersley:** Peter Minister, Digital Sculptor (tr). **108–109 Dreamstime.com:** Gemenacom (background). **109 Dorling Kindersley:** Jon Hughes (tl). **110 Corbis:** Randall Levensaler Photography / Aurora Photos (c/background). **Dorling Kindersley:** Jon Hughes & Russell Gooday (tc); Peter Minister, Digital Sculptor (tl, c). **Getty Images:** pagadesign / the Agency Collection (bl). **110–111 Dreamstime.com:** Cobalt88 (background); Deviney (inside TV). **111 Corbis:** Jim Brandenburg / Minden Pictures (br); Nick Rains (cr/background). **Dorling Kindersley:** Jon Hughes & Russell Gooday (cl); Peter Minister, Digital Sculptor (cr, tc); Jerry Young (tr). **112–113 Science Photo Library:** Mark Garlick. **113 Corbis:** Mike Agliolo (cl). **114 Dreamstime.com:** James Reid (cr). **Science Photo Library:** D. Van Ravenswaay (cl). **114–115 Dreamstime.com:** Adrian Lindley (background). **115 Dreamstime.com:** Nikhil Gangavane (crb); James Reid (cr). **NASA:** Solar System Exploration (cl). **Science Photo Library:** Prof Walter Alvarez (c). **116 Getty Images:** Jim Watt / Perspectives (bl). **116–117 fotoLibra:** Julia K. Rich (bacround); Dave Stewart (b). **117 Dreamstime.com:** Lupoalb68 (cra). **118 Dorling Kindersley:** Jon Hughes (cb). **Dreamstime.com:** Vitaliy Skigar (tr). **118–119 Dreamstime.com:** Phillip Gray (c/background). **119 Corbis:** National Geographic Society (tc). **Dorling Kindersley:** Jon Hughes / Bedrock Studios (cr); Jon Hughes (tc). **120–121 Dorling Kindersley:** Bedrock Studios (tc). **121 Dreamstime.com:** Krischam (cr). **Getty Images:** Stan Honda / AFP (b); Ken Lucas / Visuals Unlimited (cr/fossil). **122 Dreamstime.com:** Au_yeung225 (cb/skull); Natalia Kuchumova (cb). **122–123 Dorling Kindersley:** Natural History Museum, London (tc, bc). **Dreamstime.com:** Natalia Kuchumova (t). **123 Corbis:** George Grall / National Geographic Society (ca). **Dreamstime.com:** Czalewski (c); Natalia Kuchumova (cl); Anna Yakimova (tc); Vadivazhagan Margandan (clb); Winterling (cr)**124–128: The American Museum of Natural History; Bedrock Studios; Centaur Studios – modelmakers; Graham High at Centaur Studios – modelmaker; The Hunterian Museum (University of Glasgow); Institute of Geology and Palaeontology, Tubingen, Germany; James Stevenson / Donks Models –modelmaker; Jeremy Hunt at Centaur Studios – modelmaker; Jon Hughes, John Holmes – modelmaker ; Jonathan Hately – modelmaker; The Leicester Museum; Natural History Museum, London; Peter Minister, Digital Sculptor; Royal Tyrrell Museum of Palaeontology, Alberta, Canada; Russell Gooday; Sedgwick Museum of Geology, Cambridge; Staatliches Museum fur Naturkunde Stuttgart; Tim Ridley / Robert L. Braun – modelmaker.**

Jacket Images: *Front:* **The American Museum of Natural History; Bedrock Studios; Centaur Studios – modelmakers; Graham High at Centaur Studios – modelmaker; The Hunterian Museum (University of Glasgow); Institute of Geology and Palaeontology, Tubingen, Germany; James Stevenson / Donks Models – modelmaker; Jeremy Hunt at Centaur Studios – modelmaker; Jon Hughes, John Holmes – modelmaker ; Jonathan Hately – modelmaker; The Leicester Museum; Natural History Museum, London; Peter Minister, Digital Sculptor; Royal Tyrrell Museum of Palaeontology, Alberta, Canada; Russell Gooday; Sedgwick Museum of Geology, Cambridge; Staatliches Museum fur Naturkunde Stuttgart; Tim Ridley / Robert L. Braun – modelmaker.** *Back:* **The American Museum of Natural History; Bedrock Studios; Centaur Studios – modelmakers; Graham High at Centaur Studios – modelmaker; The Hunterian Museum (University of Glasgow); Institute of Geology and Palaeontology, Tubingen, Germany; James Stevenson / Donks Models – modelmaker; Jeremy Hunt at Centaur Studios – modelmaker; Jon Hughes; John Holmes – modelmaker; Jonathan Hately – modelmaker; The Leicester Museum; Natural History Museum, London; Peter Minister, Digital Sculptor; Royal Tyrrell Museum of Palaeontology, Alberta, Canada; Russell Gooday; Sedgwick Museum of Geology, Cambridge; Staatliches Museum fur Naturkunde Stuttgart; Tim Ridley / Robert L. Braun – modelmaker.**

All other images © Dorling Kindersley
For further information see: www.dkimages.com